JOURNALS OF A
Coyotero

Don Shumaker

Cover Photo by Don Shumaker

Artwork by Sharon Knight

Photo Credits—Beth Shumaker, Rue Wildlife Photos,
Linda Eanes, Craig & Dana O'Gorman, Oscar Cronk,
Mike Marsyada, Russ Carman, Jerry Brown, Torry Cook,
J.D. Piatt, Major Boddicker, James Southall,
Steve Colvin and Ed Sceery.

Book Design—Jon Marken, Farmville Printing

ISBN: 978-0-9893470-8-2

Joshua Creek
PUBLISHING

This writing is dedicated to several thousands of coyotes that I have come in contact with during my lifetime. What little I know of coyotes, after many years of study, the coyotes have taught me far more than man has, or ever will.

The author with a chicken eating coyote caught in hot weather. Operation Coyote is a statewide program (Virginia) that conducts research on coyotes and works with landowners to control problems with coyotes.

Acknowledgements

I DON'T BELIEVE I CAN EVEN REMEMBER all of the people or their names who have helped, in some form or fashion, broaden my knowledge of coyotes. Many of these people, such as Willis Kent, Johnny Thorpe, Gerry Blair and Johnny Stewart, have passed on. I will be forever indebted to them for their help and kindness, all of them. Students who learn must have good teachers, and I've had some of the best.

As far as this book goes, I have quite a few people to thank who have in some way contributed to it. My artist, Sharon Knight, is always eager to give me a hand. Dr. Leonard Rue, one of the greatest wildlife photographers (and writers) to ever exist, has been a friend and a great help to me on many of my writing and editing endeavors for longer than I can remember. Kent and Linda Eanes, Oscar Cronk, Craig O'Gorman, Mike Marsyada, Dr. Major Boddicker, Torry Cook, J.D. Piatt, Jerry Brown, Russ Carman, James Southall, Steve and Cierra Colvin, and Dr. Ed Sceery all supplied me with photos to use, and I am very grateful to them.

I owe a lot of thanks to those who assisted me in gathering information for this book. Dr. Ed Sceery, Russ Carman, Bob Noonan, Dr. Charles Cushwa, Craig and Dana O'Gorman (and Nancy), Dr. Major Boddicker, Mike Marsyada, Gerry Lavigne, Oscar Cronk, Chad Fox (U.S.D.A.) and Wayne Derrick all contributed and helped me in some way. As always, Jon Marken, my editorial consultant, helped this old backwoods coyotero by taking a box full of photos and scribblings and making a book out of it. Thank you, Jon.

My wife Beth is deserving of special thanks for her computer work, advice and for putting up with an old woodsbum who doesn't know when to quit. I think a thank you is in order to all of those coyotes who over the years have taught me much. And last but not least, I thank God for letting me live the life I have lived.

We have to both live with coyotes and control them.

Foreword

THERE IS A GROWING NEED FOR PEOPLE of all walks of life to better understand the coyote, a wild canine that is often misjudged and misunderstood. Volumes have been written about them over the years. Hundreds of studies on them have been conducted in the past 100 or so years by wildlife scientists, government agencies and private groups. Some of what I've read is very factual, some of it is pure nonsense. A few of the studies conducted on coyotes have provided us with very accurate data; many have been a waste of time and money.

Most people in these high tech, modern times are far removed from the real world of not only coyotes, but of all wildlife. I find that many of those who hunt and even a few who trap are not well versed on old wiley. People (in general) are prone to accept most anything that is written or said by supposedly "experts" as pure gospel. Many of these "authorities" on coyotes come from the professions of wildlife biologists, wildlife managers, game wardens, conservation officers, TV wildlife show hosts, anti-hunting and trapping organizations and college professors. Some of these people have high levels of education but are ignorant when it comes to knowing the real truth about coyotes. There are, however, a few of these academic professionals who have spent much time in the wilds studying, hunting and trapping coyotes. I will listen to what these people have to say.

With the coyote population in America what it is today (and

growing), there are very few people whose lives could not, in some way, be affected by a coyote or coyotes. It is therefore important that people become properly educated in this regard. What myself and others like me have learned, who have spent lifetimes studying and controlling coyotes all over North America, will be shared with the reader in this book. Our knowledge does not come from half-baked "studies," it comes directly from the coyote himself.

To be better prepared to deal with an ever-growing population of coyotes, and the problems that come with this, we have to deal in truths and facts. We are not getting much of either of these from "wildlife professionals" today. Most often, many of these people (who are being paid by us) pass on their theories, educated guesses and ignorance about coyotes to us, telling everyone that all of what they say is based on "scientific data." In this book, we will take a hard look at some of their "studies" and "facts" and then I'll let the reader decide whether to believe some of their hype or not.

While this is not a methods book on the finer details of coyote control, I will educate readers on the methods that are being used today. There are many good books and videos available that teach, in detail, control methods that really work. One can attend trappers' conventions and seminars all across America and Canada to further their knowledge in this respect. Also, there are several professional coyote control men around the country who will, for a fee, teach anyone on the fine art of controlling coyotes. When I first started trapping, 62 years ago, very little of this information was available, and like many others, I had to learn and struggle on my own in the beginning.

For those who desire to become competent controllers of coyotes, I will discuss the various tools of the trade, what works best and where to obtain such items. This is a specialized market and very few, if any, of the items needed will be found at Wal Mart or chain stores.

I have been blessed to spend much of my life running around in the wild places in pursuit of coyotes and many other species of wildlife. Much of my income and livelihood has been earned from these endeavors. I have written many magazine articles on these adventures for different publications over the years and again have been blessed to develop a number of editors and readers who like to read of these things. This book will offer some of these writings to the reader, and I truly hope you both enjoy and learn from them.

In my lifetime, following the career that I chose, I have killed several thousand coyotes. Do I hate coyotes? Heavens no, I respect and admire the coyotes for what they are and for the good that they do. Coyotes are here to stay. We have to learn both how to co-exist with them and to handle problems their presence presents. They have their place in God's scheme of things in the wild. But whether anyone likes it or not, coyotes have to be controlled. In this writing, I will explain why.

Don Shumaker
July 25, 2016

The coyote is a very adaptable creature.

Contents

Coyotes are here to stay and they do play an important role in the scheme of nature. This old boy is showing off some very impressive fangs.

CHAPTER I

Meet The Coyote

We now deal with a mixed variety of coyotes in the United States (including a part of Alaska), Canada, Mexico and Central America. The original, true species of coyotes (Canis Latrans, Latin for dog, barking) is still to be found in many parts of the country, but so many of them today are mixed with wolf, dog, or a combination of all three. Populations of these animals are stable, even growing in many areas. The eastern states in the U.S. have seen a literal explosion in numbers of coyotes in recent years.

Wolves will prey on coyotes, but there are not enough of them around to make a significant impact on them. Man is the primary predator who is responsible for keeping coyote numbers down. Diseases such as mange and rabies often kill many coyotes where populations become extremely high.

Some years ago, trappers, hunters and livestock producers in the northeastern sector of the U.S. began dealing with a much larger version of a typical coyote. They called these animals "brush wolves," realizing that it must be a cross between a coyote and a wolf. DNA studies were nonexistent back then. Now that animal scientists, researchers and the genetics people have DNA capabilities, there is an ongoing war between many of them to try and determine what is a true wolf or a true coyote. Some of these academics have renamed the "brush wolf" a "coywolf." Some say that we must reclassify these animals into different species or sub-species. Some are saying that some of the wolves found in various areas in Mexico, Canada and the U.S. are not true wolves but wolf/coyote crosses. Coyote men and livestock producers simply know that they are now dealing with pure coyotes and coyote/wolf crosses (brush wolves or coywolves).

Then to sweeten the pot and add more confusion, we have coyote/dog (domestic) crosses that are called coydogs. As a result of this mix, we now have some animals that are part coyote, part dog and part wolf! So what are we supposed to call these critters? The academics will be fighting over this for some time to come, for sure. Now that we have DNA testing to prove that many coyotes around the country have some amount of wolf genes in them, I predict that the crackpot, animal rights lovers will attempt to convince some liberal, federal judge to issue a court order to put a ban on killing or controlling anything that even looks like a coyote because they may have wolf genes in them and wolves are federally protected!

So where would that leave livestock producers? It would leave them all sucking hind tit while highly paid lawyers start their court shenanigans that could go on forever. Those of us who have spent much our lives studying and controlling coyotes know for a fact that this would be a disaster. Coyote attacks on humans and their pets would escalate, and many species of wildlife would be impacted in a very negative way.

Coyotes (pure and mixed) generally breed in late January and into February. The female's gestation period is similar to a domestic dog, about 62-63 days. Litters may average four to eight pups, al-though it is on record that one female coyote delivered 19 pups. In general, females only come into heat once a year, the heat period lasting two to three weeks. I, along with some other coyote men, believe that a female could come into a second heat if she lost the first litter. Most young females do not breed until they are going on two years old. In the wild, I have seen very few young coyote females that raised over one to two pups to juvenile or adult age and few of the older bitches ever raise over three to four to maturity.

It is said and believed by some that pairs of coyotes mate for life unless something happens to one or the other, but neither I nor anyone else has seen conclusive proof of this in the wild. One pregnant female captured near Chicago not so long ago was DNA tested, and the results showed that she had been bred by three different males. Domestic female dogs will breed with whatever mutt comes along, and I don't see a female coyote being much different.

Many people assume that coyotes (and other predators) stay in dens when they are not out hunting for food or traveling around. This is not true. The only coyotes that stay in a den are the females when they are preparing to give birth and for a while afterwards when the pups are young. The male will help his mate find and prepare a den, but she will not allow him to enter after the pups are born other than to bring food. The male, being a good father, will stay nearby and bring food that he catches to feed the nursing female and then the pups when they begin eating solid food. In all of my dealings with coyotes, I have never encountered a "dead beat dad" male coyote.

Coyote dens are, as a rule, located in hidden, secluded places that are not seen or frequented by man. In the East and Midwest, I have found quite a number of coyote dens under old, abandoned houses and farm buildings. Woodchuck or groundhog dens found along brushy streambanks and brush-choked ravines are often dug out (to make them bigger) and used as denning sites. In the west, badger holes are sometimes used as well as small caves or rock crevices that provide necessary protection and shelter. Bulldozed stump and rock piles are prime spots for coyote dens. A red fox female will take up in a den in the middle of a hayfield or in a dry culvert pipe within sight of humans, but I've never seen a coyote do this.

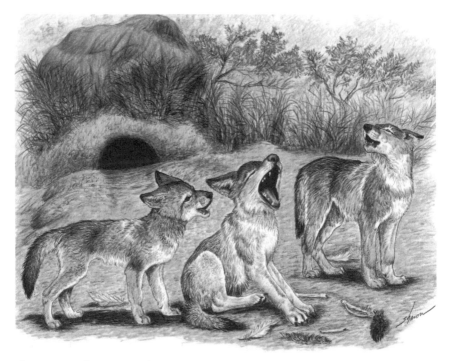

Coyote pups become vocal at an early age.

Coyotes will use the same dens year after year if left unmolested and if a good food supply is nearby. If there is any human activity up close to an inhabited den, the male and female will move the young immediately, as a rule. I have sneaked in on occupied dens close enough to put up cameras for observation purposes, and on all of these occasions, the pups were moved. Once the older ones get a whiff of man scent close to the den, they vacate, as a rule.

By the time the pups are a month old, they spend much time outside the den frolicking and playing. At the age of eight weeks or so they are weaned and start accompanying their parents on hunting trips, learning how to find food. Coyote parents also teach the youngsters how to avoid danger. They have been seen running pups away from trap sets. At this time, the den is abandoned. Studies have shown that as many as 50% or better of the pups never survive.

Young and old coyotes, quite a few of them, die from diseases such as mange, rabies, distemper and heartworms. Just as dogs do, they also battle with fleas, lice, ticks and internal parasites (worms).

The lifespan of coyotes can vary from one region to another. Under ideal or the best of conditions, coyotes can live as long as the average dog does, 10-12 years. Food supply, disease, hunting and trapping pressure, all play a role in the life expectancy of coyotes. In some areas, few live beyond three to four years old, but there are exceptions to this. I have taken some fairly old, gray-faced ones in areas where food was plentiful and they had not been hunted or trapped for years. Some of them had teeth worn down like an old hound's teeth, nearly to the gums. Where coyote populations are high around busy highways, some are killed by vehicles.

Coyotes have a very good sense of smell (ask any trapper about this). They constantly use their noses to find food and to avoid danger. Their sense of hearing is acute. The coyote's eyesight is superb. Their bodies are lean and muscular, covered by fur that enables them to withstand extreme cold weather conditions.

Skilled coyote trappers and hunters kill more coyotes yearly, all over North America, than all the other coyote's enemies combined. At times in the past, there were quite a few hard-core, professional coyote men who killed a lot of coyotes. Some of these dedicated men would take 1,000–1,500 coyotes a year, but they are few and far in between these days. The need for such professionals is there today, probably more so now than ever before, but their numbers are dwindling for various reasons that I will discuss later. Deer hunters, turkey hunters, small game hunters, farmers and ranchers kill a few, but diseases are the second largest killer of coyotes.

By the time fall arrives, coyote pups reach about one-half of their full size. Being quick learners and tireless hunters and scavengers, they can survive on their own at this time. Some of the youngsters may stay with the parents or the pack and others will strike out on their own. Quite a few of these young adults will fall victim to trappers, hunters, vehicles and disease, but many will survive and reach maturity. Some of these young coyotes that leave the family unit may travel for many miles before they settle into an area. Under ideal situations, coyotes are territorial as a rule, but a growing number of factors are changing some of this. I will devote another chapter to this subject to go into more detail.

The weight of an average coyote varies from one part of the country to another. Weight can vary a lot even in one state or region. Genetics and availability of food sources are key factors in determining what they will weigh. Coyotes with wolf or large dog genes in them will weigh more. In the east, I have caught five- to six- month-old pups that already weighed 30 pounds and more. Males will most always outweigh females. I have taken many coyotes in the southwestern area of the U.S. that weighed on the average of 25-30 pounds. I have taken northwestern and midwestern coyotes that averaged 35 pounds. In eastern states, I have trapped or shot many coyotes in the 40 to 65-pound range, most of these, of course, being mixed-gene or hybrid animals. One animal recently killed in central Virginia weighed 82 pounds! I personally handled the process of having tissue samples of this beast's DNA and tests proved that the animal was 50% coyote and 50% wolf. We are now attempting to learn where the 100% wolf parent came from. Was it a tame wolf released into the wild? Was it a northern wolf that migrated south? Though some wildlife biologists do not care for people labeling such a critter a brushwolf or coywolf, this is exactly what he was.

Coyotes are swift on their feet and are capable of running long distances. I once clocked a coyote in Arizona running alongside my truck for nearly half a mile at 35 mph. In New Mexico, while glassing a large canyon for elk, I watched two adult coyotes run down and kill a mature, healthy mule deer doe on dry ground.

Female coyotes appear to be good mothers.

Other seasoned hunters and trappers who have spent most of their lives in the outdoors have also seen coyotes run down and kill mature deer. How often they do this, no one really knows, but they are capable of doing it.

It is my opinion that the coyote is the most adaptable predator in America. I also believe that it is probably the most intelligent. I am not alone in my way of thinking on the capabilities of coyotes; many other true wildlife experts feel the same. I have removed coyotes from ranches, farms, wilderness areas, deserts, parks, swamps, villages, towns, big cities, rural country and subdivisions. They have proven that they can flourish most anywhere they care to.

Cierra Colvin, a 19-year-old lady trapper, holding one of forty coyotes she took in three months. Look out you old coyoteros, this gal may teach us something!

CHAPTER 2

A Coyote's Diet

It could almost be said that a coyote will eat anything it can swallow! One of the leading factors for its ability to adapt and survive anywhere is that its diet is wide and varied. The coyote is classed as a carnivore, primarily a meat eater, but it will also eat garbage, pet food, berries, insects, fruit, some vegetables and even watermelons. I once observed a coyote eating peaches off the ground in an orchard beside a busy highway. Coyotes are really omnivores.

Mice, voles, gophers, prairie dogs and woodchucks are relished by old wiley. Rabbits, squirrels, quail, grouse, turkeys, muskrats, beavers, opossums, raccoons, skunks, deer, foxes and bobcats are on the menu. Snakes, frogs, lizards and insects of all kinds are eaten by these ever-hungry critters. They like fish. Some learn how to flip a porcupine over on its back and eat from the belly area to avoid the nasty quills. Eggs of any kind are devoured. Some coyotes will feed on human flesh. I am sure there are other things that coyotes will eat that I didn't mention or am not aware of.

Thousands of sheep, lambs, calves and small pigs are killed and eaten by coyotes in North America every year. Now, having said that, I will add that many more thousands of these same domestic animals are eaten by coyotes that were not killed by the coyotes. They died of natural or accidental causes and merely provided an

The author has watched two adult coyotes run down and kill a grown, healthy deer on dry ground. Where the snow piles up, they can really hurt deer populations.

easy meal for old wiley. But in many cases, the coyotes will get the blame. Coyotes often get blamed for livestock kills made by dogs.

Not so long ago I responded to a supposed coyote kill and carefully examined the carcass of a 500-pound steer. There were no bite marks anywhere on the animal, and I told the cattleman that the steer had died of other causes, unknown to me. He got a bit perturbed at me and insisted that coyotes killed it. I also told him that if coyotes had killed this animal, they would have eaten on it. I asked him why he was so sure that coyotes did the dirty deed. His answer was that he had been hearing coyotes howl on his place! I have looked at hundreds of calf kills made by coyotes, mostly newborns, but I have never seen any real evidence of even a pack of coyotes killing a steer this large.

On the other end of the spectrum, I have responded to livestock loss calls and the people have told me that a game warden or someone who worked in the office of the game department told them that coyotes very rarely ever killed livestock! So you see, we have untruths being spread in every direction by people who know absolutely nothing of coyotes or their kills. The coyote often gets the blame for kills he didn't make and then gets a free pass on some that he did make.

More and more these days I get calls from people living in rural and urban areas where coyotes were seen coming into a yard or on a porch killing and making away with house cats and small dogs. Coyotes are opportunists and will take advantage of an easy meal whenever they can. I have also witnessed where coyotes killed and ate small hunting dogs that had strayed away from their masters or while trailing or running game. Coyotes will kill dogs that are treeing game up a tree when the opportunity arises.

I am amazed at the number of people these days who think they can turn their chickens out to range and forage without losing any of them. There are a number of critters out there that love chicken meat—hawks, eagles, owls, foxes, possums, coons, domestic dogs, mink and, of course, coyotes, to name some of them. Then we have the tame duck and geese folks who feel the same way. I have, on more than one occasion, seen where coyotes ripped apart pens and cages of flimsy wire (such as poultry wire) right in people's backyards to get a fowl or tame rabbits. Never underestimate a coyote's capacity for bold acts when it wants to fill its belly.

A landowner/hunter that I trap for told me of an incident that reinforced my outlook on how bold a coyote can be. Early one morning, during the black powder rifle season for deer, he turned his flock of prized Rhode Island Red laying hens out to free graze and headed out on foot to a nearby tree stand. About an hour later, a coyote that held a still-flopping red hen in its mouth raced past his tree stand, and he never even got a shot at it! That's pretty bold, I would say.

Coyotes all over the country kill and eat a lot of deer, especially fawns. Some wildlife biologists still attempt to downplay this fact, for reasons I don't know, other than maybe being ignorant to the real truth. On the other hand, coyotes eat a lot of deer meat that they don't kill. Road kills, deer crippled by hunters and those that are sick or die of old age provide old wiley with a lot of tasty grub. In some areas of the country where deep snows force the deer herds to "yard up" to survive, the coyotes kill many of them. In the northeastern states, such as Maine, the larger-than-average, wolf-cross coyotes can really hurt deer populations.

In other parts of the country, especially in towns and cities, the coyotes actually help the deer herds by helping to keep them thinned down to a sustainable level. I constantly hear many deer hunters complain about coyotes killing all of their deer, and in many of these situations I have seen that deer numbers have dwindled somewhat because of loss of habitat, a poor food supply, diseases and excessive harvests. But the coyote gets the blame. In areas where deer numbers are really down, coyote depredation can hurt the chances of the herd repopulating tremendously.

It takes a lot of groceries to keep a coyote strong and healthy. When food is easily available, they will eat in large quantities. All of the coyotes I have ever skinned were well muscled and trim, with the exception of a few very old or sickly ones. I have never seen a healthy, skinny coyote. When you look at what is on their menu to eat, it is easy to see why we see very few malnourished ones!

If it is your desire to hunt or trap coyotes, remember this. The successful coyotero goes to where the coyotes get their groceries! On farms in the Midwest and East that raise chickens, turkeys and hogs, the coyotes will visit these places looking for dead birds or animals that have been composted or thrown out. Anywhere in the country where cows are calving in pastures, the coyotes will be there, eating afterbirth and looking for the opportunity to snatch a newborn calf. Wherever there are sheep, the coyotes will surely be nearby. In the Southwest country where there are often extremely

The author with two calf-eating coyotes.

high populations of rabbits, I found many coyotes. The coyotes will always be found where there is food for them.

I once trapped a farm for several years that had a huge old persimmon tree located in one of the backfields. Coyotes, foxes, coons and possums love persimmons, and I always caught two–three coyotes and several foxes each year near that old tree. Where there are persimmon trees, you can bet that most every coyote in the country will know where they are.

Both parents of coyote pups teach them how to survive.

CHAPTER 3

Coyote Facts & Fiction

O NE OF THE PRIMARY PURPOSES for writing this book was to educate all people, hunters, trappers, livestock producers, government wildlife officials and the general public about coyotes. There is far more fiction being spread around these days about coyotes than there is truth and facts. Sad to say, most of the fiction is being spread around by government wildlife officials and those people in academic professions who supposedly "study" wildlife. There are also a fair number of hunters, trappers and livestock producers who also contribute to the telling of untruths about coyotes. And let's not leave out the TV show "wildlife experts" who would have us believe that they are all knowing.

It is human nature for many people to want to impress others with their great knowledge on a subject. It is commonplace for government officials on all levels to want to be authorities on subjects that pertain to their line of work. These people feel the need to have to give an answer for any question that is put before them. Real, honest-to-God coyote men such as myself and others I have known are not ashamed and do not hesitate to say "I don't know" when asked some questions about coyotes! Many of us have made our living studying and dealing with coyotes, often 365 days a year, and we realize that there are some things about coyotes we will probably never know.

Often, I have listened to people from all walks of life spout off about coyotes. I have watched TV shows, read most of all the books on coyotes and the lengthy, written "scientific studies" performed by well-educated academics on coyotes. It has never failed to amaze me and other coyote men about how utterly naive and ignorant many of these people are on the subject of coyotes!

Before I go into specific examples of coyote facts and fiction, I will explain to the reader how so much of this erroneous information evolves. We will take a look at how and why untruths about coyotes are passed down through educational institutions throughout the land and are accepted as the gospel truth.

Bear in mind that it is not my intent to badmouth or condemn all wildlife professionals. In my many years of traveling around the country, I have met some very knowledgeable, open-minded wild-life people who had what it takes to successfully seek and find the truth about coyotes and other species of wildlife. These people had academic training, a lot of field experience and, most importantly of all, common sense and the ability to reason. They were not afraid to question their academic professors or the higher-ups in the wildlife agency they worked for. My hat is off to these people, and I have learned from them. These people were smart enough to know that just getting a degree (or degrees) in wildlife management did not make them an instant expert.

Government wildlife agencies on all levels have spent millions of dollars over the years on what they refer to as "scientific" studies. "Scientific data" is gathered to complete their studies, and then they come out with what is regarded as truth and fact. Sometimes, they do actually find truth and facts. Very often, however, their studies may somewhat add to their knowledge of the species being studied but do not actually prove anything as positive fact or truth. I have been told by some wildlife professionals that studies are sometimes conducted in a manner so as to support a preconceived theory!

Coyotes kill a lot of fawn deer all over North America.
Where deer populations are too high, this can be a good thing.

Now why would they do that? Well, it could be for any number of reasons. One, they want to convince people to believe what they believe, even if they can't really prove it. Some want to be regarded as absolute, all-knowing authorities. Some of these studies are conducted for political reasons and are used to convince others to go along with their agenda when setting wildlife management regulations.

For a number of years now, the animal rights folks who are against killing anything have had a growing influence on people in America, even those who are paid by the people to manage wildlife. When I have told some who work for wildlife agencies that some in their ranks are anti-hunting and trapping, they acted a bit astonished and argued with me. Some even got angry. But if you open your eyes and see what's going on, you will see that what I say is the truth.

A good morning's take of Arizona coyotes by the late Gerry Blair and myself.

Many wildlife studies have been conducted by people who were not qualified to do it. But in the end, their "findings" are regarded and accepted as the truth that is not to be questioned by a mere farmer, hunter, trapper or landowner. These untruths are passed down to the next generation of wildlife scholars, and after some time, a lie will be accepted as truth. You don't dare question the all-knowing authorities.

Knowledgeable coyote men search for real truth and facts. We have no political agenda to pursue, nor do we have to agree with questionable "facts" in order to get a passing grade and get a degree. We seek to learn all we can about coyotes because it is what we are—coyote men. It is what we do for a living. Although they are constantly searching for answers in regards to coyotes and their behavior, coyote men are realistic and honest enough to admit that there are some things they will never know about coyotes. They do not promote or believe in half-baked theories and SWAGS (scientific, wild–assed guesses). The really sad part of all of this is that probably 90% of those who work for and run our wildlife agencies look down their educated noses at real coyote men and disregard nearly everything we share with them and the public. We are not "trained wildlife scientists"!

Rarely do I even argue with the academics anymore; it's not worth my time. I do, however, attempt to educate the general public about coyotes, especially those who call on me who are having problems or issues with coyotes. I will discuss some of the more common false or fictitious statements that are going around that are put out to the public by wildlife officials and others. I will share with you what I and other coyote men with years of experience dealing with and studying coyotes have to say. I will leave it up to the readers to draw their own conclusions.

"Coyotes prey on the sick, old and crippled animals. Rarely do they kill healthy, mature adult animals."

What a joke! A coyote is a very accomplished predator/killer that consumes a lot of groceries of all kinds and will kill anything that it can kill and eat. They do this every day, either singularly or in pairs, groups or packs. I have seen two coyotes run down and kill a mature, healthy deer. Others have seen this also.

"Coyotes don't generally kill livestock or other domesticated animals unless there is no other food around."

This statement, often told by wildlife officials (including some game wardens and conservation officers), is another pure lie. Coyotes expend much less time and energy killing a newborn calf, a sheep or lamb or a small house dog than they do trying to run down a rabbit. A coyote must eat and will eat whatever it can get, anywhere, anytime.

"Not all coyotes are livestock killers. We should only remove those that do kill livestock and leave the others alone."

Any coyote is capable of killing livestock and will do so if the opportunity arises and it does not fear for its own safety. On numerous occasions, I have watched a coyote (or several of them) pass near or through a herd of cattle (with calves) and not attempt to bother them. Why? Because they are smart enough to know that they cannot fight off a herd of angry cows. If that same coyote or coyotes come upon a small calf away from the protection of the mother or the herd, you have a dead calf—guaranteed!

Now I have a question for the wildlife scientists. Unless I see a killing and can positively identify the killer, how will I know which coyote to trap, snare or shoot? How do I determine a good one from a bad one? Even the best of the coyoteros would have a hard time pulling this off. There is no way that I can keep the non-killers out of my traps, so should I just let them continue to kill livestock? Perhaps the government should set up a "coyote court" to determine who's guilty. Maybe someone can develop a lie detector machine to use on coyotes to get the truth out of them. Or perhaps we can construct a "coyote breathalyzer" gadget to be able to tell whether the critter has been eating mutton or beef!

"If you kill one coyote, two will come to replace it."

I have heard this one quite a bit lately, and it is about as absurd as you can get. Coyotes are constantly dying off or getting killed. If two came and replaced every one that dies, wouldn't there soon be coyotes standing on top of coyotes? Also, I'd like to talk to the people who actually stayed out there in the woods and saw this happen. Who are they? Coyote populations are constantly fluctuating because of many factors that come into play.

"When the pressure is on and more coyotes are killed, the remaining females have larger litters of pups."

Some years ago, a couple of animal scientist/researchers did a limited study on coyotes and came up with the above conclusion or theory. The animal scientific community ate it up and began

Coyotes slaughter thousands of sheep annually.

teaching this as 100% gospel in wildlife schools. It has been repeated so much that even some fairly good coyote killers believe
it. The two originators of the theory have since admitted that they
were surprised at how well this theory caught on. Those that are
opposed to coyote control love it because it gives them a supposedly
"true scientific finding" to use against controlling coyotes.

"Denning" for coyotes is an old method of reducing coyote
populations. Coyote men use various methods (howling, dogs, etc.)
to locate dens and destroy the pups. I have found coyote dens in
areas where myself and others had drastically cut coyote populations and the liter size was one to three pups. How could this be?
Shouldn't they have had eight to ten pups? I have found dens in
areas where coyotes had never been controlled up to that point and
the females were nursing large (eight to ten) litters of pups. It just
didn't go along with the great coyote litter theory, and other coyote
men told me they had observed what I had. Should we dare question the educated ones on their conclusion?

Now, for real facts. Researchers and coyote men have learned
that the younger females, especially those with their first litter, have
fewer pups. Older female coyotes in their prime generally have the

largest litters. Of course, these findings can change when we encounter and factor in a lot of variables.

"We must learn to live with coyotes. If we leave them alone, they will control themselves."

This one takes the cake. I have either heard or read about this one constantly in the past year. When I first heard it, I almost threw up my last meal. Several hundreds of thousands of sportsmen or taxpayer's dollars have been wasted to come up with such an absurd, ridiculous statement or finding. In my opinion, it is one of the better examples of government waste and the spreading of information that has no merit.

Yes, we have no choice but to live with coyotes; they are everywhere and are here to stay. But we must be realistic and know that they have to be controlled. To say that coyotes will control themselves is absurd and preposterous. The game departments set seasons, limits and regulations to control deer and other game species. Why would a coyote be any different? Coyotes have no other major predator than man, are very adaptable and have proven that they can live and thrive anywhere, which tells me that control for them is far more necessary than for many other species.

Some say that game department officials favor the presence of coyotes because they help control deer populations, especially in urban areas where they are often considered to be pests. Some say that automobile insurance companies favor them because they kill deer, which could lessen the number of deer/car crashes. I really don't know what game officials and insurance companies say about coyotes in closed door meetings, and they will probably never tell the sportsmen, the landowners and the public of their true thoughts anyway.

For some years now, there have been discussions about administering some sort of birth control measure to coyotes. Much of this has come from the animal rights advocates, and it wouldn't surprise me if some of the game departments are not looking into it also. They could waste a lot of our money on mere "scientific studies" in this area. Perhaps they could leave condoms throughout the land for the male coyote to use?

All across America, millions of dollars are spent annually to control dog populations. Dog wardens and animal control officers are constantly chasing after millions of unwanted dogs and puppies. Anytime a female dog comes into heat, she will breed if she can and the dog control problem continues on and on. A coyote is a canine and is no different in this respect. So how do animal scientists figure that coyotes will control their own numbers? Often when their numbers reach very high levels (due to inadequate control measures), diseases such as mange or rabies will knock their numbers down temporarily. I have wondered if the animal scientists consider this as a part of coyotes controlling themselves?

Food supply and availability often control how many coyotes can live in any given area. Coyote men have known this for years. They also know that when food becomes scarce in an area, many coyotes will move on to other areas where there is food. They don't stop breeding because of food supplies! Consequently, we have seen coyotes move into and thrive in every type of habitat and environment in the land. And the population of coyotes continues to grow. They do not, and will not, control themselves.

"Coyotes rarely attack or kill humans."

Not so long ago a young, grown woman was hiking in a Canadian park, and several coyotes attacked and killed her and then fed on her flesh. More recently, a young child was snatched from her yard in California and killed. Go on Google and type in "coyote attacks on humans" and see what comes up! The numbers of coyote attacks on humans is on the rise and will continue to rise as both human and coyote populations increase. Anyone with plain old common sense can see that happening.

Myself, I don't walk around in fear of coyotes attacking me, even though I spend most of my time in areas where there are coyotes. But I do know that coyotes will attack (and attempt to kill) people under certain circumstances. That is a fact that we have to live with. If more coyotes were killed, the number of attacks on humans would decline. Another common-sense deduction. Because they are not often hunted, trapped or killed in city and urban areas, coyotes lose their fear of people and problems will surely stem from this.

"If coyotes aren't killing your livestock, leave them alone. If you kill these 'good coyotes,' they may be replaced by 'bad coyotes' that are livestock killers."

This statement was made to a group of cattle farmers by an official representative of the U.S. Department of Agriculture recently. Here again, I am dumbfounded by the high level of ignorance that is often found in many of our government officials and "experts"! But on second thought, I wonder if this guy was really that ignorant, or did he just want to discourage these cattlemen from pestering the U.S.D.A. for help in controlling coyotes, a job that they get paid to do? Either way, it's a sad situation.

Like myself, many of the good coyote men that I know read about all of these "scientific studies," and most often we are torn between whether to laugh or cry. One of my old buddies (who spent a lifetime studying and controlling coyotes) once told me that what really angers him about these studies is that they insult the intelligence of all of us who know anything about coyotes. On the other hand, these researchers dazzle many game department officials, sportsmen and the general public with their bull crap.

My good friend Terry Huskey holds one of many coyotes I've caught on his hog farm.

*The late Gerry Blair, my old coyotero partner and mentor
with a single coyote I called in and he shot.*

CHAPTER 4

Coyote Packs, Pairs and Singles

ONE COLD, DREARY AFTERNOON, I let go of a coyote howl in the Carson National Forest in central New Mexico and the response from coyotes was immediate. Three groups of coyotes began yipping, yapping and howling all around me, and they were close. I was a veteran coyote caller but must say that I was caught off guard. This definitely was not the norm.

I sat down on a large rock with a scrubby juniper at my back, affording me good cover. The coyotes were coming together out in front of me, still yapping at each other. In the next few minutes I counted at least 20 different coyotes, and I'm positive there were more. They milled around smelling each other and barking and then vanished into the juniper growth, going in all directions. One headed my way and I shot it.

Never have I seen that many coyotes together before or since. I have often pondered over that incident and finally came to the conclusion that these three groups or families of coyotes just happened to be at the same place at the same time, and I was just lucky enough to witness the event. Those of us who have spent our lives in the woods have seen some things that we simply can't explain.

So many people think that coyotes always travel in packs, but this is not true. People constantly tell me about hearing packs of ten or twenty coyotes howling on their property. In reality they have

From the puppy stage on up, most coyotes are very sociable animals.

heard three, four or five coyotes yipping, barking and howling that make enough noise to sound like twenty. When I tell people this, most of them look at me like I'm nuts, and I've learned to let them think what they wish.

As a whole, coyotes are social animals, and yes, they often do hunt and travel in a group at times. Most of these groups consist of a family of coyotes — the father, the mother and two or three younger ones. Sometimes several other coyotes may join up with them for a while. But these same coyotes often split up in pairs or singles and hunt. In my opinion, there is a simple reason for this. A rabbit, woodchuck or other small animal will barely feed one coyote for one day. Competition for food can be keen at times for coyotes. The actual edible meat found on a deer fawn or lamb may feed two coyotes for a day. Singles or pairs of coyotes may hunt on their own for one night or several. Then after a bit of howling to locate each other, they will again come together as a group or pack. When large carcasses such as grown deer, elk or cows are found, the group will then feed together until it is all gone. As with wolves and other larger predators, there is most often a pecking order existent among the coyotes to determine who eats what and when.

What many people don't understand is that coyotes cannot survive for long in large numbers on a limited amount of ground or range. Half a dozen coyotes, if they traveled together constantly, would probably kill each other over food. The coyote is a very capable hunter and forager and can be a very vicious and ruthless killer. Forget about what the all-knowing educated ones are telling everyone about "good coyotes." Any single coyote has the potential of killing anything it can get its mouth on when the opportunity presents itself.

Years ago, I had a trapper friend in one of the western states who raised a coyote pup. Even after reaching maturity, the coyote was as good a pet as any dog I've seen. His master fed him the best of food and actually spoiled the animal, but he would pounce on and kill every chicken, duck, turkey and housecat that he came upon. He once tore the wire off the kid's rabbit hutch and ate the tame rabbits. One of the kids asked the father why the coyote would do this when he couldn't have been hungry.

"Because he's a coyote," the father replied. "It's what he does and he can't help but follow his God-given instincts. He'll always be a coyote first and anything else second."

Several times in my life I have been fortunate enough to observe coyotes actually hunting in a pack. The devils would fan out like an accordion when on a track or just hoping to flush out unsuspecting quarries. At times, they would come in close to each other but then spread out again if the situation deemed it necessary. When a kill was made, then the feasting started.

When coyotes pair up to breed and raise a litter of young ones, they will quit traveling with the pack or group altogether. Once a den site is selected, the other coyotes, for the most part, keep their distance. Both the male and the female will hunt from the den area, and once the female gives birth, the male does most of, it not all, the hunting for food. Once the pups are big enough to move around, the female will venture out short distances from the den. While working on coyote control jobs for livestock producers, if I caught a nursing female in a trap, I knew the den and the pups wouldn't be far off.

Many years ago, in Arizona, I observed a strange occurrence among some coyotes that I never have been able to explain. It was one of those beautiful, bluebird days in the high desert country that made a man mighty glad to be alive. I had started out before daylight that morning, cruising the back roads and stopping to howl every two or three miles just to see how many coyotes would respond to my handcrafted cow horn howler that my friend Herb Brussman from up in Oregon had made for me. Herb was one of the real, old-time coyote men that I've always had a lot of respect for.

The howler did everything I thought it would do, and I was very pleased with it. Before the sun heated the country up too much, I decided to climb up on a high, rocky point and just take in the beauty and smells of the desert. I had my binoculars with me and started looking over the country that stretched before me. It wasn't long before I spotted some movement out directly in front of me about 200 yards and focused in on a large, male coyote trotting along with what appeared to be a dead rabbit in his mouth. The coyote ducked into a brush-choked, rocky ravine and I lost sight of him. I knew there would be a den somewhere in that ravine.

Scanning over the area, I spotted another coyote, a smaller one, with something in its mouth approaching the rim of the ravine from the opposite direction. It, too, ducked down into the ravine, and I was wondering what the heck was going one. Had the female ventured out a bit and caught a pack rat or small bunny? A minute or two passed, and then I heard one of the coyotes give out a few coarse, short barks. The smaller coyote popped up out of the ravine,

Dr. Ed Sceery in New Mexico with a good take of coyotes.

stood for a moment looking around and then trotted off out of sight among the greasewood brush and cactus. I was (and still am) thoroughly confused at what I had witnessed.

Later that year I shared this story with Wiley Carroll, a legendary coyote and mountain lion chaser from Nevada. Wiley's take on it was that the smaller coyote was a son or daughter from the past year's litter that had not wanted to stray far from the parents. This explanation was about as good as anything we could come up with, but I'll never know for sure.

Like some people, not all coyotes are social creatures. Many times, in my career as a coyotero and a student of old wiley, I have come across singles or pairs that lived pretty much to themselves. Why this is I don't really know, but I suspect that their individual personalities cause them to be this way. Quite often I have responded to coyote damage problems where one single coyote hung around a place picking off free-ranging chickens, barn cats or ducks, one at a time. Once that one coyote was removed, the killing stopped and no other coyotes were caught, seen or heard in that area.

This big male hombre wouldn't take kindly to a newcomer invading his territory.

CHAPTER 5

A Coyote's Territory and Range

HERE IS A TOPIC THAT MOST animal scientists, biologists and even some trappers think they have all figured out. By adorning a few live trapped coyotes here and there across the country with radio tracking collars, they can tell us for certain how far a coyote ranges or how big his or her territory is. The interns or students, working under the guidance of a scientific guru from some game department or university, diligently tracks and records these coyotes' movements and travels on maps. More often than not, these "scientific studies" are made possible by grant money that came from the taxpayers' pockets.

After the study is completed, the results are written up and presented to all other wildlife officials and the general public—these scientific facts will go down in history and will be used and repeated by other wildlife officials for years to come. No one, especially someone from outside the academic circles, should ever question the validity of such studies. Often those who conduct these studies will be given awards and praised to high heaven.

I don't know of any professional coyote men who is against studying and learning more about coyotes. Hell, that's what we have been doing for much of our lives, often on a year-around basis. Our livelihoods have depended upon learning as much as we can about coyotes in order to control them, as needed, more efficiently.

Just like a domestic dog, male coyotes urinate on objects to mark their territory.

So we are not against learning from anyone. But we do question and even resent many of these "scientific studies" that are conducted in such a manner that really don't prove much of anything, or they only confirm much of what we have already known for years! We resent many of these studies that twist the truth and are used to spread false information to enable these "experts" to carry out their own agendas.

Based upon my own experience with coyotes over a long period of time, I'll make these statements about a coyote's range or territory. Any coyote will travel as far as necessary in order to survive. I have never found a coyote (a healthy one) that starved to death.

If the groceries get scarce in say a five-square mile area that he has been living in, then he will go ten or fifteen miles in order to eat and stay alive. If hunting or trapping pressure becomes intense in the area or territory where he has been living, and he sees some of his family and fellow coyotes getting killed, he will move as far as necessary to survive. This could be a temporary or a permanent move. The distance moved could be two miles or twenty. Rarely will we ever know for sure.

Science, good old reasoning and common sense have clashed many times and will continue to do so as long as man is on earth. Brilliant scientists have tried for centuries to convince us that man evolved from an ape. Some have bought into that theory, but those of us who still can think for ourselves, who use reasoning and common sense, believe in God and what the Bible teaches us. Real coyote men know that all or some of those radio-collared coyotes could have left that territory at any given time, during or after the study. We know this because we have seen it happen many times. We also know that there were probably more coyotes in that same territory that weren't caught and collared, and we know that we will never know what those coyotes did.

Food supply is what I believe determines, for the most part, the size of a coyote's range or territory. And we know that food supplies and sources can and do change, sometimes in a short period of time. Changes in the habitat that provides shelter and cover for coyotes can also play a part in how far a coyote roams. As I mentioned previously, hunting and trapping pressure can affect the range and movements of coyotes. Weather is sometimes a factor.

Coyote populations, a topic that I will discuss in the next chapter, also play a part in how far coyotes will range. When there are fewer coyotes, they usually don't have to travel as much to eat well. But when populations rise and the land will not sustain but so many (carrying capacity), they may have to travel long distances to find food. On one hog farm that I trapped over the years, it is normal to catch ten to fifteen coyotes off this five-hundred acre farm each year in a month's time. If I left traps and snares out year-around on this place, I'd probably catch double that number. Not many of these coyotes are living year-around on this small farm. Some are traveling long distances to eat hog meat.

Some coyotes that have been radio collared traveled many miles before they settled down on a place or were killed. Why? There really is no way to answer this for certain. The coyote could have been run out of some of the territories he crossed by resident coyotes. As I mentioned before, some coyotes are not as sociable as others. Some are just loners by nature. There is no way of knowing how far some of these coyotes travel in their lifetimes, and we will never know if they ever stay in any area for long. No amount of scientific study, even when it is conducted properly, will ever give us all of the answers to questions we have. The hard-core coyote men who chase after coyotes year around don't have all of the answers either, and most of them will admit that they don't.

Coyotes in North America have expanded their range from sea to shining sea in recent years, and there is nowhere else they can expand to unless they charter boats and move into Europe and other continents. If coyote numbers are reduced in an area for what-ever reasons, there are plenty more nearby to fill the void. No, they don't control their own numbers as some researchers and academics would have us believe. And we didn't have to spend thousands of dollars of someone's research funds to determine that. We have learned what we have by being out there with coyotes many hours, many days and most of our lives.

Many people do not realize that the academics or "professionals" do not consider what real coyote men see and have learned to be of any real consequence. They regard the information that we have gathered—even the cold, hard facts—as "anecdotal." Even if we

Jerry Brown (R) and a Texas friend with a lassoed coyote.
If it can be done from the back of horse, Jerry can do it!

conduct studies in the very same manner as they do, our studies are not considered to be real, of any value and certainly not "scientific." If you are not one of them, what you have to offer is of little or no importance. This doesn't apply to just studies and information on coyotes, it applies to all other species of wildlife. These people are hell-bent on being the final authority and having the final say. I think that maybe ego and job security have something to do with this attitude.

A black coyote taken in Virginia by coyoteros Kent and Linda Eanes.

CHAPTER 6

Coyote Populations

WITH THE EXCEPTION of a very few places in North America, coyote populations are on the rise and will more than likely continue to rise. There are several reasons for this, and I will share them with the reader. My statements are based on facts, the truth, not scientific theories. I keep in touch with some of my old coyote killing buddies around the country, and they tell it like it is. If they say coyote numbers are on the rise in their area, you can believe it.

The few places where the coyote populations are stable and not rising are primarily the small areas where real coyote men are hired to kill coyotes. There are also a few, select areas in a handful of western states where coyotes produce a very desirable fur or pelt that fur garment manufacturers want to buy. These areas see more pressure on coyotes since a handful of dedicated trappers and coyote hunters take a fair number of them (as long as the fur prices make it worthwhile).

Craig O'Gorman of Montana keeps the coyote population down to a manageable level and livestock losses are minimal (more on this later) in the country where he is hired to control coyotes. He has worked this same area for many years, and his work has saved livestock producers many thousands of dollars. John Graham is a full-time coyote man in Wyoming, and his efforts and hard work keep the numbers of coyotes down there. On cattle and sheep farms

As coyote populations rise, so does the need for food to feed them.

where I have been paid to control coyotes (on a yearly basis) in Virginia, livestock losses (from coyotes) are very low, even non-existent on some farms.

The problem is, there are fewer O'Gormans, Grahams and Shumakers out there as each year passes. And there are fewer part-time or hobby coyote hunters and trappers out there who used to kill maybe a dozen or two each year. Low fur prices paid for coyote pelts in most parts of the country have caused many to hang up their traps, snares and guns. Another factor that comes into play is that there are fewer young people taking up hunting and trapping in general. Trappers, who are the primary controllers of coyotes, have seen their ranks steadily decline for years. And it's not just about money—most young people these days do not want the hard, sometimes miserable work that goes with trapping.

Another reason why coyote numbers are going up is that the devils have adapted very well to living in close proximity to man. They now live (and thrive) in towns, cities and urban areas where it is very hard for even experienced coyote men to control their numbers. I have tackled a few of these jobs, and they are difficult and no fun at all. These areas provide sanctuaries where the coyotes can reproduce well, and the new coyotes overflow into the rural areas, where there are already too many coyotes and very few, if any, coyote men. Does this sound like "coyotes control themselves" as some would have us believe?

Millions of acres of public lands in several western states have been shut down to trapping in any manner that's good for controlling coyotes. The animal rights activists, inside and outside of state and federal game agencies, are responsible for this fiasco. This has been a situation (like many others in the U.S.) where the minority has ruled. Sound wildlife management practices have been thrown out the window. The government buttholes that are in cahoots with these animal rights nutcakes should be fired, tarred and feathered!

With little or no hunting or trapping pressure on coyotes found on these millions of acres, their numbers will increase to high levels. Most all species of other wildlife will suffer from this. More and more of these excess coyotes will be forced to move to nearby private lands, where livestock losses will rise. Some of these coyotes will take up in city and urban areas where they will have an even safer place to reproduce. Ignorant town and urban dwellers will even feed the cute, hungry coyotes! Rabies, mange and maybe a couple of other diseases will be the only things that will knock their numbers down some, but it won't be enough. Coyote attacks on humans will continue to rise and thousands of pets will be eaten.

I am constantly approached and questioned by people who know what I do for a living. I truly like to share what little knowledge I have of coyotes (and other wildlife) with folks, and hopefully I do

Coyotes kill and eat a lot of housecats in rural and urban areas.

educate a few of them on the true facts about coyotes. But I must
admit, there are times when I grow mighty weary of this, especially
when I encounter those who say they want to learn and very quickly
let me know they know it all about coyotes. Hell, they learned
everything they needed to know off the computer, a TV show or
some game department brochure. Some of them, those who really
want to learn the truth, have asked me why can't the people who are
being paid to manage wildlife see what's going on with the coyotes.

Here's my take on that question. There are a few government
wildlife managers still out there who know the truth and what
needs to be done. My hat's off to these people and I respect them.
But the majority of the people who are now in charge of managing
wildlife and setting regulations and control policies are ignorant in

this respect and don't know the truth! Since their first day in college they have been brainwashed by a group of professors who don't have a clue about managing coyotes! These professors pass on the same erroneous bullshit that some professors or "wildlife expert" taught them. But they know they are right because their information came from "scientific studies" conducted by their own peers or cronies.

I have known a few government wildlife officials who did "see the light" after some time. Some of them quit their cushy jobs in disgust, but most of them stayed on and went with the flow because they didn't have the backbone to dispute their peers and superiors. As a result of this fiasco, the general public is fed a host of untruths and misinformation about coyotes, and many believe it! You cannot convince many of these gullible people that some who work for the government are ignorant, dishonest or both.

Another question about coyote populations that I am often asked is, "How many coyotes are in our county?" Now if I were with the academic crowd, the answer would be simple. Wildlife officials in many states will say that there is roughly one coyote per square mile. That seems to be a pretty universal thought or theory. Truth of it is, it's a simple guess.

My answer to people on this question is that I nor anyone else really knows. I can tell them about how many coyotes I caught or killed in a certain area, and that's about it. And that's truth and fact, not theory or a guess. Why would I want to lie to these people? Only God could tell us for sure how many coyotes are in a certain area at a certain time. Anyone who tells you any different is feeding you a line of bull.

Over the years, I have conducted some of my own studies trying to determine how many coyotes were in an area. I did this in several states, east and west. I am very familiar with how the academics conduct these population studies, and I duplicated their methods and procedures. I employed scent stations, counted droppings, re-

When coyotes become overpopulated, diseases such as mange often crops up. This is a slow, torturous death.

corded tracks and actual sightings. I called and howled for coyotes on a systematic basis several times a year. In fact, I think I put more into my research than most other researchers would, and I also had an edge by being a longtime coyote man who was very familiar with their travels and habits.

Now, because I don't have a degree in wildlife biology or management, my studies would have been deemed as "anecdotal" or irrelevant had I gone public with them. But I conducted these studies to see if I could really learn more about coyotes and if I could accurately give a number of how many coyotes resided in or used a certain area.

The results? I learned that I could not say how many coyotes there were per square mile in this area or even how many actually passed through the area. Without all of the "scientific research" work, I could have made one pass through the same area and confirmed that several coyotes passed through this area. I also confirmed my hunch that these animal scientists were blowing smoke and were attempting to impress people with their "educated" guesses. They can only give us "SWAGS," scientific wild-assed guesses!

A good coyote man can spend some time in any part of the country and tell if there are hardly any or no coyotes using the area, if there are a few coyotes using the area or if a lot of coyotes are using the area. If he goes beyond that, he may have started blowing the same smoke that the academics do.

Not so long ago, I removed 15 coyotes off of four farms that were spaced about a mile apart, a total straight-line distance of about six miles. In the adjoining county, I ran another line of traps and snares in an area about three times that size and removed 39 coyotes! That's a lot of coyotes from such small areas. I've seen and experienced much in my sixty years of trapping, but these catches surprised me.

I had trapped all of these places for four or five years in a row and usually averaged about half or less as many coyotes in the same area. Because I keep good records of my catches, for my own information and for the landowners, I could see that less than 20% of these coyotes caught were juveniles less than a year old. I checked all of the females carefully and found that about half of them had raised pups that year, none of them having large litters. Landowners have told me since I pulled up from those areas that they have seen a coyote here and there, so I didn't get all of them.

So why so many coyotes in such small territories? Where did they all come from? My guess is that some of these coyotes came to these farms from other areas because the calving had started. They relish eating afterbirth and are always looking for a chance to grab an abandoned, young calf. Perhaps the supply of fawn deer and small prey that they had fed on in other areas had been eaten up.

My guess or hunch on this is based upon what I know can happen. I do not know this for a fact, nor could anyone else say for sure.

Rob Erickson, an expert on city-dwelling coyotes, removes and studies coyotes living in the city of Chicago and surrounding villages and urban areas. I am truly amazed at how many coyotes are thriving and multiplying in such areas. He recently told me about removing four lactating females from a five-acre lot located adjacent to a large hospital! You can bet there was a male or two somewhere nearby. Add up the females, the males and a few pups, and you're looking at maybe fifteen to twenty coyotes roaming around in a small area. Of course, some of them will die and some will move to other areas. I wonder where and how they get enough to eat.

The bottom line on coyote populations in the U.S. is this—no one knows for sure how many there are roaming around. Nope, I can't tell you nor can any academic. We can only make educated guesses. I can tell you for a fact how many coyotes I killed in a certain area, and the numbers are most often far more than what wildlife officials would have claimed or guessed were there.

Coyotes have keen eyesight, hearing and sense of smell.

Coyote's Song

It is a symbol of all that
is wild, the coyote's song.
It may come in a staccato burst,
or it could be mournful and long.

They have been hated and
scorned by many, loved by few,
But they have persevered and
flourished, no matter what we do.

Man puts food out in front of
them and dares them to eat,
But old wiley likes nothing
much better, than tender red meat.

The trappers go after them
and make much ado,
But some of them catch
none, some catch only a few.

Many living things will leave
this earth, they will all be gone,
But those that are left here
Will still hear the coyote's song!

Coyotes howl for a multitude of reasons

CHAPTER 7

Coyote Vocalizations

I N MY LIFETIME OF TRAVELING AND WANDERING in the wild places all over North America, I have had the enjoyment of listening to many coyotes vocalizing. The utterances, yaps, yips, barks and howls of coyotes have always held me somewhat mesmerized. When I hear coyotes, I stop and listen, always trying to figure out what they are talking about. With some of the haunting sounds they make, I have a good idea of what's going on; with some I don't.

*Champion coyote caller Torry Cook can imitate any sounds a coyote
makes using mouth blown calls. He also uses Icotec electronic callers.*

I have been around some people, many of whom are professed
coyote experts, who claim to know what's happening anytime a
coyote open its mouth. Then I've accompanied a few coyote men,
ones who have spent their lives studying and controlling coyotes,
admit that they, like me, were sometimes baffled at the meaning or
purpose of some coyote sounds. There are many things about wildlife of all kinds that I've seen or heard and simply cannot explain.
Regardless of how much they are studied, coyotes will always keep
us guessing to some extent.

Many times, on TV programs or movies I've heard wolf howls that were supposed to be coyotes howling. If you ever hear a wolf howl and then hear coyotes, you'll easily see that there is a vast difference. In recent years, however, I have heard mature male coyotes whose howl was almost a mix of a coyote and wolf. Quite a few of these critters I killed, and know from putting my hands on them that they were a mix of coyote, wolf and sometimes with a little dog thrown in. All of these coyotes were taken in the eastern part of the U.S., but I'm sure there are some of the same sort of critters roaming all over North America. A few other coyoteros whom I have great respect for have heard the same, but wildlife academics and educated professionals will pass off what we have seen or heard as anecdotal. The reader can believe whomever he or she wishes.

There are about five sounds that most coyotes make that are somewhat universal and generally intended for the same purposes. The first one is the plain old howl, high-pitched and drawn out. Sometimes these howls are preceeded by a yip or yap or two. I have heard these same howls followed by a coarse bark or two. A coyote's bark, when it barks only, is generally considered a sound of warning, which has often had me questioning the bark/howl combo. One theory I have entertained is that an older male's bark and higher-pitched howl is intended for the same purpose as a younger coyote's yip and howl. The same goes for females.

This howl (with or without yips or yaps) is considered by coyoteros to be sort of a "I'm lonesome" howl. Some people call it a "locator" howl, a howl made to locate other coyotes. I think that it is made for both reasons. When we attempt to locate coyotes in an area for any reason, this is the sound or howl that we most often use. We use our own voices, a mouth-blown howler or an electronic howler to put this sound out there and see if we get a reply. If we get a reply or several of them, we know for damn sure that coyotes are nearby. If we don't get a reply, we may assume there are none within hearing distance, but this assumption can very often be wrong. For reasons unknown to us, coyotes will not answer our howls on many occasions.

Let's move on to the coyote bark, which is a short, gruff bark. When you hear a coyote doing this, you can be almost certain that he or she is excited, spooked, angry or all of the above. Coyote barks are a warning to other coyotes that something is amiss. Many times I've had coyotes hide back in the brush and bark like hell when I approached one of their kind that was held in a snare or trap. I have never heard one give an honest-to-goodness "lonesome" type howl in one of these situations. But I have heard quite a few give a quick series of barks and attach a short, abrupt howl to the last bark. Coyotes will sometimes bark warnings when danger in any form comes near an active den of young coyotes.

Yips, yaps and a host of other similar sounds constitute much of the noise we hear from coyotes. These sounds are often a mix of different pitches, and the longevity of them varies. We most often hear this medley of sounds when several coyotes are together. Often one or more coyotes will add in a high-pitched howl along with this racket. Get five or six coyotes going together on these choruses and it can raise the hair on the back of your neck! I have often referred to these erratic combinations of coyote sounds as a chorus performance put on by the hounds of hell.

Coyote men often refer to a "ki yi" call. Simply put, this is the sound of a coyote in pain or distress. If you have ever heard a dog cry out in pain when someone stepped on his paw, you've heard a ki yi call. With various styles of mouth-blown predator calls, coyote hunters often mimic a puppy making this squealing sound to lure coyotes into shooting range. It can be very effective.

The last coyote vocalization that I will discuss is the challenge howl. This a short, often rough-sounding howl made by a coyote that warns strangers to stay off his turf. Sometimes he will let go of

two of these short howls close together. Sometimes a gruff bark will be included. It is believed that the alpha male of a pack or group of coyotes is the one that makes this howl. I believe that any mature male coyote will make these howls on occasions. I don't know if a female coyote ever makes a challenge howl.

Many times I've heard coyotes yipping and yapping as a team or group when chasing down prey. Once I observed a female (mother) coyote yip and howl to attract her half-grown pups to come to a dead cow she had found. Coyotes can make sounds that are hard to describe, and I have no idea what message they convey to other coyotes. They also growl and whine when occasion calls for it.

Near the end of this book there is a chapter devoted to information on where the reader can learn more about coyotes from books, magazines and videos. Some of the videos include all of these sounds, and you can hear what they are like. I also encourage those interested in this topic to spend time outdoors to get the sounds straight from the coyote's mouth. Coyotes will make any of these sounds at any time, day or night, whenever some occasion prompts them to do so. A wailing siren going down the highway will often cause them to break into a melody. Years ago, I had a pack that roamed near my place in Nebraska that would yip and howl in response to a train whistle.

I don't believe that we will ever know about all of the sounds coyotes can and will make. But it sure has been an enlightening and interesting experience for me to try and learn more.

Coyotes can be very aggressive.

They are beautiful animals and have a purpose here on earth, but they have to be controlled.

CHAPTER 8

Who Controls Coyotes?

FOR MANY YEARS, fur trappers and hunters have harvested more coyotes than any other group of people. But as I mentioned previously, with a dying fur market (worldwide) and fewer people taking up the art of chasing coyotes, this group of people will be taking fewer and fewer coyotes. For a century or more, various federal, state and local government trappers eliminated many coyotes, but this has changed also. Though the U.S. Department of Agriculture currently employs a few trappers scattered around the country, from what I have learned they have not hurt the coyote population much. State, city and county trappers are nearly nonexistent today.

Hired, private coyote men take a lot of coyotes, but there are fewer and fewer of these men each year. One of the reasons for this is that few people want to pay them what their work and efforts are worth. Most state game agencies do not want to hire control men, nor do they want to pay private contractors to do this work. They bitch and moan about their budgets, but many of them waste millions of dollars on projects that are absolutely unnecessary and useless. Much of their spending is wasted on things that provide very little, if any, benefit to wildlife and sportsmen. Many game agencies (on all levels) have become so political (and politically correct) that they are sickening, to say the least.

Livestock associations, especially those located in the western states, are the largest employers of professional coyote men. But as livestock producer numbers shrink (especially sheep growers), the number of coyote men shrink also. This leaves old wiley in a very good position to raise more of his own kind and do more killing. The killing never stops; coyotes hardly ever miss a meal.

There are a few competent coyote men who trap for private stock producers on an "as needed" basis all over the country, but here again, very few farmers and ranchers want to pay them what they need to make to survive. Some (a very few) well-heeled hunt clubs and game preserves will sometimes hire a coyote or predator control man. I personally know quite a few top-notch coyote men who have given up the profession altogether and have had to seek other employment to support themselves and their families. These men will be extremely hard to replace. There are still quite a few people around the country today who trap a coyote or two for recreation, and some who call and kill a few coyotes for sport, but real coyote men are fast becoming a vanishing breed. I have known a few U.S.D.A. trappers who were real pros, but I've seen some who weren't worth the paycheck they drew.

Most of the old-time government coyote men (on any level) were good at their jobs. They somehow lived on starvation wages but were dedicated coyote and predator control men who got the job done. These men killed thousands of coyotes and loved what they did. We don't see many of those types of people working any government jobs anymore. I am truly thankful that I got to know and learn from some these old characters before they passed on.

Since I moved back to Virginia after spending quite some time out in the wild west, I have gotten a few thousand calls from people wanting help with coyote control. These folks ranged from livestock producers to pet owners who lived in towns and suburbs. Deer hunters, rabbit hunters, chicken growers and people from all

Coyotes are great hunters/scavengers and can be very intelligent.

walks of life have sought my assistance. I was unable to help most of them simply because they didn't want to pay me enough to cover my gas bill, much less make a living! I have killed a few coyotes in my life, and it's not like I want to impress anyone with my abilities as a coyote man, so why would I work at something that costs me money?

Folks in the eastern part of the U.S. are just beginning to catch on about coyotes. People out west have had to deal with them for years and are more aware of what they are dealing with. I'd now like to share with the readers how the coyote episode or drama has unfolded in the east in recent years. Being an old coyote man, I've had a front row seat to this show.

I now reside in the foothill country of the Blue Ridge Mountains in Virginia. Virginia is a mid-Atlantic state that has everything to offer a coyote that he or she needs. The state is well-watered with millions of acres of brushy country and thickets that offer coyotes a lot of cover. The state is covered with many livestock farms (cattle, sheep, hogs, chickens, turkeys) that provide a never-ending source of food. Wildlife abounds throughout the state, and deer populations are excessive in most parts of the state. This state has very few trappers and hardly any real coyote men. It is a mecca for coyotes. Virginia (and other eastern states) have what it takes to sustain a much larger population of coyotes than some of the larger western state I've lived and operated in.

When coyotes first appeared on the scene, people were naturally concerned and began to question the wildlife authorities. "Oh, don't worry about coyotes," they were told. "They only eat mice or sick, crippled or road-killed deer and hardly ever bother livestock." I've had many concerned people who called the wildlife experts for help with coyotes tell me this. "We can co-exist with coyotes with no problems," they were told. These gullible people were (and still are) being advised about coyotes by authorities who hardly knew one end of a coyote from another! They merely repeated to these people what they had heard, or recited something written by other academics who didn't know about coyotes either. The people trusted these professionals they were paying. Why, they were the "experts," weren't they?

Well, time went on and the coyote population increased rapidly, for there was little in the way of control put on them other than an occasional hunter shooting one or some trapper who caught a few for the novelty of it. I pretty much sat back and watched the drama unfold. When people who knew I had experience with coyotes asked me about what was going on, I told them my thoughts and what I'd seen, for what it was worth. I trapped very few of them simply because their fur value was next to nothing. It was not worth my time and effort.

After some time, the crap began to hit the fan. Farmers started losing valuable livestock, homeowners saw their pet dogs and housecats being killed and eaten by coyotes and deer hunters began to notice that very few doe deer had fawns by their sides. A man cutting his lawn on a riding mower was attacked by a rabid coyote. Almost overnight the coyote went from being an interesting novelty to a vicious beast that needed to be exterminated! Game department officials worked (when forced to) at calming people down, and that's when we started hearing that there were "good" coyotes and "bad" coyotes. We only needed to control or weed out the bad ones and "co-exist" with the many good ones! The coyotes would eventually control their own population, the citizens were told.

U.S.D.A. trappers were being sent here and there to take out "bad" coyotes. I'm sure they were successful at not killing any "good" coyotes. Hell, these boys worked for the federal government so they had to be "experts," didn't they? State game officials were happy because they had the U.S.D.A guys to pass all these coyote problems on to. Why, in the year 2015, the U.S.D.A. reported that six of their trappers had removed 512 coyotes from Virginia at the mere cost of roughly $775.00 per coyote! Alas! The federal calvary had rushed in to save the settlers.

Now that I have given both the game department and the U.S.D.A. trappers in Virginia a hard time, I will now come somewhat to their defense. In regards to our game department, they did change our snare regulations in order to allow trappers to be more efficient at taking coyotes. Not all of the departments' employees are as brainwashed or narrow-minded as some when it comes to the need for coyote control, and this is a step in the right directions. Game department statistics show that hunters and trappers reported killing 1,295 coyotes (statewide) in 1993-1994, and the number reported in 2008-2009 was 24,449. I feel safe in saying that double that many were actually killed.

While the U.S.D.A. had six trappers working on coyote control at times, none of them worked at it full-time. They often had these same guys working on all sorts of other problems and programs. Six professional coyote men working year around on coyote control can take five or six thousand coyotes per year (total) where coyote populations are high. U.S.D.A. trappers in Virginia only responded to a small number (191) of farms that were either experiencing livestock losses from coyote predation or were in eminent threat of predation. These trappers did not have the time to hang around and kill all of the coyotes they could; they usually pulled up stakes as soon as the killing of livestock stopped.

Killing 512 coyotes did help farmers reduce their livestock losses, help they may not have gotten from any other source. Another factor that limits the amount of help the U.S.D.A. boys can give livestock producers is that of funding. They can only provide as much as they have funds to pay for. Livestock producers need to put pressure on legislators to help remedy this problem. Those that raise food to feed America should be high on the list to receive any form of aid that will help them stay in business, as long as funds are not squandered.

Myself and other knowledgeable coyote men and wildlife managers predict that the coyote problem will only grow in America unless measures are taken to hire professional coyote men in all areas of the U.S. to keep the numbers down. And it's a known fact that those in the private sector can and will provide superior service for less money. County, state, city and federal government agencies can hire these people and save taxpayer dollars while providing a much-needed service.

Cierra Colvin is working overtime to become a coyote specialist.

*Without any control measures taken on them,
coyotes overpopulate quickly.*

CHAPTER 9

Effective Coyote Control

THE FEW THOUSAND SPORT HUNTERS and trappers scattered around the country who kill 1-100 coyotes per year are to be commended for their time and efforts. A fair amount of game and livestock are saved annually due to their endeavors. But this is not effective coyote control. The coyotes are multiplying at a much greater rate than they are being taken.

Professional coyote and predator control men, whether working as private contractors or as government trappers, are needed to effectively control coyotes. While a part-time operator (private or government) can stop the killing of livestock on a farm or ranch or two for a short period of time, this will only be a temporary fix. Those of us who have spent a lot of days working with coyotes (and the problems they cause) know that the only true way to effectively control coyotes is to reduce their numbers significantly, across the board, in every crack and corner where coyotes exist. We have never bought into the "good coyote, bad coyote" bullshit and never will! We know that any coyote is capable of killing anything at any time when the opportunity presents itself. Yes, some coyotes probably live and die without ever killing livestock, but many of these just never have the chance to. And you can bet that these "non-killers" still breed to produce some offspring that will kill livestock. Plain common sense tells us that fewer coyotes will prey on fewer victims.

Even if you do have a Ph.D. in wildlife, you can't argue that one and win.

I would like to share with the readers some examples of effective coyote control. Keep in mind that these are true, factual accounts and the numbers are real. These are not based on studies or theories, nor are they thoughts or opinions that have been passed down for generations. I hope you will see the "proof in the pudding," so to speak.

Before L. Craig O'Gorman took over the predator control program in 1975, the sheep men of Powder River County, Montana, were losing around 3,000 sheep a year to predation. In the year of 2016, 30 lambs and 15 ewes were lost by the sheep men in Powder River County. How could this be achieved? What happened?

The people who know anything much about Craig O'Gorman will tell you that he has been one of the most dedicated, hardworking and persistent coyote men who has ever killed a coyote in North America. His goal has always been to be the best coyote man in the country. Not only did he learn all he could from many of the great, old-time coyote men, he is a very innovative individual and a high achiever. I've always noticed in my own long career as a trapper that the better trappers are both driven and obsessed with it.

Craig used every tool and method known to man to control coyotes, 365 days a year. Traps, snares, calls, decoy dogs, poisons, denning and aerial gunning cost many a sheep killer in the Powder River County his fur. If the tools he used were not the best for the job, he came up with better ones. His wife, Dana, makes and sells some of the best animal baits and attractors a trapper can buy.

The Craig O'Gorman/Powder River County saga or story is hard, indisputable proof of what effective coyote control can accomplish. No, the coyotes that Craig dealt with didn't learn how to control their own numbers, nor did they all become "good" coyotes. They became dead coyotes! And I can bet you that there are still ample numbers of coyotes in that part of the country. Craig nor anyone else will ever eradicate all of them.

James Southall is a hard-working young man who took the job as farm manager for a 1200-acre livestock farm in the central part of Virginia several years ago. Both sheep and cattle are raised on the farm, and when the young man took over the farm, coyotes were murdering the livestock on a grand scale, especially the sheep. James was interested in trapping and learned about coyote control from a U.S.D.A. trapper and other coyote men that he got to know. He instituted a year-around program to kill coyotes on the place using foot traps and snares.

In four-and-a-half years, James killed 97 coyotes on the place, and predation dropped sharply during that time. If he had killed coyotes for only one or two years, the killing of livestock would have again risen to the high, record levels and gotten worse each year. Here again is hard proof of what consistent coyote control can do to save livestock.

The experience that James has had on the 1200-acre farm also takes us back to the topic of coyote populations and ranges or territories. If you average out his coyote kills over the four-and-a-half years he's been on the job, it comes to over 20 coyotes killed per year. Could 20-plus coyotes live on or even pass through that size farm (per year) in an ordinary situation? I think not. The high numbers of sheep and cattle on the place draw many coyotes from long distances. Territorial boundaries mean little to hungry coyotes in search for an easy meal. Other farms trapped near this one produced the normal three to six coyotes per year, so this proves to me that not all of the coyotes that James killed came from close by.

My records show that all of the farms that have employed me to control coyotes have seen sharp decreases in the number of livestock animals lost due to coyote depredation. Over a five-year period, calf losses to coyotes have dropped from 12 calves to zero on one farm. On another farm, the loss of sheep has dropped from over fifty ewes and lambs to an average of six or eight. Yes, there are still coyotes hanging around these farms and always will be, but as long as the coyotes are controlled on a regular basis (not just when killing gets out of hand) these places will experience fewer losses. That's a fact, learned by spending much time out there with the coyotes and keeping good records. But because guys like myself, Craig and James are not academic types, working for some form of government as a regular employee, all our information will be considered by the academics as "anecdotal," not "scientific." What a joke! Many of these academic professionals (guys and gals) simply refuse to admit that there are others out there who know more about coyotes than they do. I think it's mostly a control and ego thing with them. How sad.

I have never known any real coyote pros who gave a hoot in hell about what others thought about them to any great degree. None of them ever have to worry about job security as long as coyotes continue to breed (if someone will pay them). Awards and fame (other than those that come from other coyote men) mean little to them as they are not concerned with impressing the general public. These types of men are content to be able to make a living out there with the coyotes and other predators. They strive to be good at their job, but they are not known to be people pleasers.

Wayne Derrick, a well-respected coyotero and predator man from southeast New Mexico, used to kill upwards of seven hundred coyotes a year when he worked as a U.S.D.A trapper. That's effective coyote control. Like other coyote pros, he realizes the need to kill coyotes on a consistent basis, year around throughout all of the territory he's working, not just hot spots that are experiencing livestock losses.

Effective coyote control requires persistence and good coyote men who consistently kill coyotes wherever they can. Some academic experts came up with a theory sometime back that unless 70% of the coyote population is removed, control is ineffective. Livestock producers and real coyote men have had a lot of laughs over that one, but you wouldn't believe how many wildlife managers bought into that crap. Anytime you remove any number of coyotes from any area, livestock and wildlife will be saved. Here's a question for the oh-so-smart academic ones—if you don't really know how many coyotes are in an area to begin with, how in the hell do you know when and if you've killed 70% of them? We'll go a little more into the 70% theory later in this writing.

The coyote trap held by young Austin Seay costs over $20.00 each.
The cost of coyote control continues to go up.

CHAPTER 10

The Cost of Effective Coyote Control

WHETHER ANYONE LIKES IT OR NOT, it costs money to control coyotes. And the costs to control will rise in coming years, I guarantee you. As with other things we deal with in life, we will get what we pay for.

Many animals that need periodic or constant controlling can be controlled effectively much cheaper than coyotes. Why is this? Well, coyotes are, for the most part, intelligent canines who learn fast and soon become more difficult to catch or kill when control measures are taken against them. The costs of equipment alone needed to catch or kill coyotes is far more expensive than say equipment that's used to kill groundhogs. I have taken 230-plus groundhogs on a 1,000-acre farm with traps that cost four dollars each in a couple of weeks. It could take me a half a year or more and I would travel hundreds of miles back and forth to kill 230-plus coyotes in 20-dollar traps.

Even the best of coyote men can kill only so many coyotes in a day or a year. There have been days when I harvested ten or twelve coyotes, but there have been many days when I took none! Overall, if I were paid a decent amount for each coyote killed or so much a day for wages and expenses, I would probably average two to four coyotes per day. That I have done for extended periods of time in my career as a coyotero. But think of this—I worked long hours seven days a week and traveled thousands of miles. Many miles traveled equals many dollars spent in a vehicle, gas and equipment. If I didn't get paid well or if the sale of the furs didn't go well, I lost money.

Most all professional coyote men or other animal damage control (ADC) trappers love (for the most part) what they do. Many of them could make more money doing other things, but they choose the business of trapping, hunting, controlling and studying coyotes or other critters (beaver, skunks, lions, bears, foxes, raccoons, etc.). And that's what it is for them, a business that hopefully provides them with an income to live on.

About all of the hobby, part-time or sport trappers I have known hope to make enough money from their efforts to at least pay for their expenditures. Some do, many don't. But they do it because it is their preferred hobby or sport. They love it. Part-timers kill a lot of coyotes, especially if the demand for coyote fur is good and prices are high.

But all in all, it most often will take full-time coyoteros, killing year around, to really control coyotes effectively. These men are, for the most part, much better at the game than many of the hobby boys. They have to be or they wouldn't be in business long, as a rule. By doing what they do, day after day, year after year, it is only natural that they see, experience and learn more and become more efficient coyote killers. Now I have seen a few so-called professional coyote men who were about useless in their work for government agencies as employees. You can bet that they got and kept their jobs by who they know. I also know quite a few part-time coyoteros who would make very good professionals if they chose to do so and had the opportunity.

Starting out on the high end of the scale on what it can cost to remove coyotes, I know of one fellow who has been paid over $3,000.00 to remove a coyote from a big city. From what I've read

Animal Damage Control expert Steve Colvin spends a small fortune annually in gas controlling coyotes and other varmints.

in government reports, each coyote the government boys catch can cost the taxpayers from $700 to $1,500. The most I've ever been paid to catch a coyote is $1,500.00, one that was roaming an urban area, eating cats, small dogs and terrifying the residents. Very few coyote men ever get paid these high figures to remove coyotes.

Going to the lower end of the pay scale, many coyotes have been killed or trapped for absolutely nothing. This is where the sport hunters and trappers come into play. Some of these do skin coyotes they kill when the fur is "prime" (cold weather months). Depending upon the fur market at the time and the quality of the fur, some pelts may fetch five dollars while some may bring more than one hundred dollars. Many part-timers never bother with the skins, es-

*Coyotes are savvy critters who learn fast. I used a bird feather
dipped in lure to get this calf killer, an old female. It can often cost a
heap of time and a lot of money to remove troublesome coyote.*

pecially in the warm weather months when they are worthless.

Some trappers will catch coyotes for free because the landowners
will let them trap other furs found on the land that may be bringing
decent money. Sometimes coyotes are killed for free in exchange for
the privilege to hunt or fish on the place. These arrangements work
out well for both parties concerned. However, with a depressed fur
market and with fewer people taking up the art of trapping and

the older ones having to quit (or pass on), there will be fewer and fewer free coyotes killed in the coming years. Coyote populations will climb and predation will increase, creating a demand for more private coyote operators (paid) or more government trappers.

How much does a private, pro coyote man need to charge to make a decent living? Well, if he was paid by the number of coyotes removed, he would have to get paid around $250.00 per coyote. If he killed 500 yotes a year, that would gross him $125,000 per year. Deduct vehicle and equipment expenses and the guy might net somewhere around $60,000–70,000 a year. That may sound like big wages to some to get paid for what you like to do, but there's more to it. A guy getting paid this much would basically be on call seven days a week. And then he would have to pay for his own life and health insurance for himself and maybe his wife and kids. When you figure that this man will work at lot of 60–70 hour weeks, the rate he is earning on an hourly basis shrinks considerably.

Many men, young and old, have talked to me wanting to do what I've done for a living. Quite a few have tagged along with me wanting to learn the ropes and go on their own. I can count on one hand how many of these guys have become pro trappers and hunters and stuck with it, out of many. In the beginning, these people have no idea how much work is involved. The high-rolling coyotero will work in extreme heat, extreme cold and everything in between. He will work in mud, snow and dust. His truck will eventually be wrecked or beat up from having to travel rough, treacherous roads.

I can remember several newly planted, thriving vegetable gardens that went to weeds and waste because coyote problems demanded that I be on the road from before daylight until after dark. I've had to cancel many fishing trips, cookouts and other activities because of coyotes. Many times, I've hated to hear the phone ring when I had just sat down to a nice dinner and didn't want to talk to anyone. I have become aggravated by people who wanted to talk about coyotes forever when I stopped to get fuel or coffee. I've had confrontations with animal rights activists and had people tamper with or steal my catches and equipment. When some wise guy even hints of me getting paid "big money" to play in the woods, I get pissed!

There's another unpleasant thing that sometimes comes with the coyotero's job. You are often under pressure to stop the killing and produce coyotes, regardless of existing conditions. Most people regard you as the pro, the guru of coyote control. You are supposed to produce both miracles and dead coyotes almost instantly. You are getting paid to produce; you're not a hobby trapper who doesn't have to produce. There will always be a jerk here and there who will badmouth your work no matter how well you do your job.

When I first started working as a coyote man in the private sector, I had a lot to learn about dealing with people (not coyotes). Now there are many landowners, farmers and ranchers I have worked for who were great people and became lifelong friends. Then you have the butt holes. Most of the butt holes I've had dealings with in my coyote work were arrogant, wealthy people.

Years ago, when I was a younger coyotero attempting to get my feet on the ground and build my reputation as a pro coyotero, I would jump at the chance to take any job. One day a fellow called me who was having problems with coyotes killing calves and sheep about fifty miles away, and I made haste to meet with him. I do remember that the man had already lost eight calves and about twenty or so ewes and lambs. This was a considerable loss in dollars, not chump change, and the killing would continue if control measures weren't taken.

I arrived at the sprawling estate and pulled up to the huge mansion, and the owner came out to meet me. Without much of a courteous greeting, a "thank you" for coming out or a handshake, the man began rattling off to me about having fired one trapper who couldn't stop the killing and that he would pay me $50 for every coyote I killed. I asked him who the trapper was and he told me. I knew the trapper, knew he was a decent sort but also knew he didn't have much experience with coyotes. He was a good beaver trapper and a fair fox trapper, but he was out of his league here.

I explained to the man that I couldn't make a go of it at the rate he wanted to pay. I told him I'd have to get at least $150.00 per coyote or charge him $100.00 per day for a 10-day period. He responded by saying that he'd pay me $75.00 per coyote or a flat fee of $500.00. He was only willing to do that because he was desperate and I came highly recommended. He also commented that he didn't appreciate folks attempting to rip him off just because he had a lot of money.

Oh, I both wanted and needed that job some kind of bad! But I could feel the red creeping up my neck and I was beginning to really not like this hotshot. I had learned enough at this point in my career to know it was better to sit under the shade tree at home or on the river bank fishing than to spend a lot of money on gas and work my butt off and lose money. I thanked him, told him I couldn't help him and began walking to my truck.

"Where are you going!" he yelled at me. "I need your services now—don't walk away from me!"

I stopped, turned and replied, trying my best to keep cool. "Mister, with what you want to pay and with your attitude, you and your livestock and your coyotes can go to hell." I got in my truck and left him standing there, cussing me. The whole affair ruined my day.

About a week later, "Mr. Rich" called me one night and said he wanted to apologize for his previous encounter with me. He told me he had done more research on this "coyote thing" and he had talked to other livestock producers whom I'd worked for in the past. He said he would be glad to pay whatever my fee was. He had lost two more calves and more sheep.

I really did need the income and I killed coyotes for him. If memory serves me correctly, the killing stopped after I killed three coyotes on the second or third night after setting up his place. I killed four more coyotes after that and left the traps and snares out for several extra days, but my job was finished. I told the man that he probably wouldn't have any more trouble until the following year. His calving and lambing was over with, and any other coyotes that may have been around were thoroughly spooked. The old codger tipped me a hundred dollars when we settled up, and we remained friends until he passed away. I trapped for him (and some of his rich friends) for several years.

I went into detail explaining about what a coyotero has to contend with not just to fill up book pages, but for a purpose. Some people who read this book will be in need of the services of a pro coyote man. These people need to realize that a real coyote man has spent years learning his craft; he's a true specialist. Just like a good mechanic, an accountant or an electrician, he deserves to be paid well! Most of us don't drive shiny new trucks and we don't dress like we just came out of the Orvis shop, but we are true professionals and expect to be treated and paid as such. For those of you who are considering a profession as a coyotero, you need to know what you're getting into and what it takes.

Clink, the German Terrier, was good at locating coyote dens.

Farm manager of Brooklyn Roads Farms Mike Randolph
hoists two calf eaters they paid me to catch.

Who Should Pay for Coyote Control?

THIS IS A CONTROVERSIAL TOPIC and one that I feel sure will be even more so in the future. Coyotes reside everywhere and their population grows. They are not just pests to livestock producers and wildlife sport hunters; their presence is beginning to affect other people as well. I have given some insight on what it takes to effectively control old wiley and how much it can cost. So the big question is — who will pay for it?

I can't count the number of times I've heard someone say, "They need to put a bounty on those damn coyotes!" Well, my answer to that are questions of my own. Who, exactly, is "they"? The government? What agency of what level of government? Should livestock producers foot the bill? Sportsmen? Taxpayers in general?

I have often heard game wardens, wildlife biologists and others in wildlife management tell people that a bounty system on coyotes has never worked and never will. There is some truth to that, but most of the people who make that statement do not have a clue about the whole truth that surrounds coyotes and the bounty system. Like other myths, half-truths and outright lies these same people feed the public, their answers are not based upon any real experience they personally have had with this controversy, they come from the "professionals" who in the past have formulated statistics and "scientific data" to encourage people to believe what they say!

Properly run and managed bounty systems on any animal can (and have) decimated their numbers drastically, or they can result in the extinction of a species if carried to extremes. I guarantee you that if a bounty of $250.00 for each coyote killed was paid across the board all over the United States, coyote numbers would be lowered within two years to a very manageable level. If it lasted longer, coyote numbers would become very low and stay low. Depredation on livestock would be near nonexistent.

There are several reasons why a bounty system on coyotes (anywhere) may have failed or appeared to fail. The primary reason for this is simple—not enough was paid for each coyote killed. I have operated as a coyotero in some areas where a bounty of $25.00 to $50.00 was being paid for each coyote killed. If stock producers or others were not paying me a fee also, above and beyond the bounty money, I would not have been there. Why? Because no coyote man, a professional who earns his living at taking coyotes, can make a living on bounties alone that are that low.

When the amount of bounty being paid is low, most of the bounty money will be collected by part-timers, hunters and landowners who would have shot or trapped these same coyotes anyway! A bounty system such as this will be, more or less, a failure. It will not reduce coyote numbers significantly, enough to do any real good, and is doomed for failure from the start.

Wildlife officials are often quick to say that a major reason for the failure of bounty systems is the mismanagement of funds being paid out. They tell how some people will collect on the same coyote more than once. I'm sure this has happened. But I ask you, is this the bounty system's fault or does it rest on the shoulders of those administering the program and paying out the funds? To me, the way I see it, this is an admission of guilt by government officials that they, or some of their own kind, are not competent or honest enough to run such a simple program! Through ignorance of true

Ask anyone who should pay to control coyotes and you will get many different answers.

facts or for ulterior motives, these real "experts" will forever spread this misinformation to the public and other government officials.

To place all of the financial burden of controlling coyotes on livestock producers would be unfair, I believe. Yes, they are the ones who suffer most (financially) from coyote depredation, but how about the folks who lose pets, even a child, or those who are attacked by coyotes? How about hunters whose wildlife populations (those animals that coyotes prey on) decline? The number of people who are being (or can be) affected by out-of-control coyote populations are increasing each year while our wildlife managers, as a whole, sit back, ignore the problem and do nothing substantial to correct the problems caused by old wiley.

Some people will argue that none of their tax money should be spent on coyote management because they don't raise any livestock, they don't have pets, they don't hunt, and because they live in a high-rise apartment, their children will never be attacked by a rabid coyote. One of my thoughts on this is that there are millions of tax-payers who never had children who nevertheless have contributed much (through their tax money) to the funding of schools! Much of my tax money has gone to support wasteful government programs that I resent or that I personally will never benefit from. What's the difference?

What I am going to say next will anger many government folks, especially those involved in wildlife management. No government-run agency is capable of running an efficient coyote control program without help and guidance from outsiders, private coyote profes-sionals. In fact, no government agency or person should ever have full control over such a matter if it is to be successful! Overall, most government attempts at coyote control for the past one hundred years or so have been failures. Why is this? I believe the primary reason for this is simple. We have not had real, knowledgeable people who have had enough "down in the dirt" experience with controlling coyotes heading up these programs. The average aca-demic or political type person has no idea of what is needed to get the job done. Political correctness, peer pressure, personal feelings and fear of the anti-hunting/trapping people control or greatly affect decisions made by many wildlife managers today, even some of those who have some knowledge of effective coyote control.

I have never known or heard of a professional coyotero who backed down from the anti-types. However, I have seen this happen many times when government folks are attacked by these fruitcakes. Many are afraid of losing their jobs, many want to be "loved" by everyone and some are simply spineless. Why should these types of people be in charge of any program or have any say in developing policy for these programs? Those who work in wildlife management and have their heads on straight, those who see the truth for what it is, rarely climb the ladder and have any real positions of authority. Seems to be the American way anymore, especially in government sectors.

Ranchers and farmers throughout the county who are getting assistance from U.S.D.A. trappers are getting much-needed help with their coyote problems. But there are many who do not for various reasons. One, the U.S.D.A. does not receive enough funds to hire as many full-time coyote men as they often need, especially in the east. Secondly, some livestock producers may get help that is not as good as it could be for a host of reasons. Keep in mind that the U.S.D.A. is funded with tax dollars, so why shouldn't they receive enough funding to effectively control coyotes as they need to be rather than operate as they are now, doing only a part of the job? Also, remember that it costs taxpayers about triple (or more) the amount to kill a coyote under the U.S.D.A. system than it would if private contractors were doing the same work. And then some question the situation where private individuals must compete with their own government, people whom they help to pay.

Currently I am seeing more folks who must hire someone for coyote control or either learn how to trap and shoot coyotes themselves. If they are not in a position to do either of these, they are out of luck and must endure whatever problems the coyotes create. Unless a viable, efficient and effective coyote control program is put into effect with necessary government funding, I predict that the coyote problem will only get worse and cost everyone more in the future. This could be avoided if the right people in government would get their heads out of the sand and if citizens would pressure politicians to do what is necessary.

*The author used a mouth blown predator call
to lure in and kill these two coyotes.*

CHAPTER 12

Methods of Coyote Control

THERE ARE SIX BASIC METHODS used to control coyotes. These are trapping (using foothold traps and snares), calling, running with dogs, poisoning, hunting over bait and aerial gunning. On a limited basis, there are places where hunters will surround an area and others drive the coyotes out to the shooters. Of all the methods used, trapping is by far the most widely used and accounts for the largest percentage of coyotes killed annually. Denning for coyotes, the act of locating pups in a den and killing them, was a popular method of coyote control used in western states in times past, but I don't hear of much of it being done now.

The art of trapping coyotes with traps or snares is one that requires a fair level of expertise. Good equipment must be used as coyotes are strong animals and can be hard to hold. The best coyote traps are not cheap, and along with the other equipment needed, a beginning coyote trapper can easily plunk down $500.00 to $1,000.00 just to get started on a small scale. If an aspiring coyote trapper hesitates about buying the best of equipment, he or she should never attempt it.

When using foot traps, the trapper has to be capable of getting the coyote to put his foot on a small piece of metal (the trap pan) about 1½" across in order to make a catch. In order to snare a coyote, the trapper must know how to get the animal to pass his head through a 12" loop (or less) of snare cable. Now when you look at the hundreds and thousands of acres that any coyote can roam, you can easily see that a competent coyotero has to know his stuff! This if not a skill that can be acquired in a short period of time. I believe I can safely say that less than 10% of those who give coyote trapping a shot end up being competent, effective coyoteros. Coyote trapping can provide one with many frustrating experiences, even when you are good at it.

In my writings, I often refer to foothold traps. These are what we use these days to catch and hold coyotes. These traps catch the bulk of coyotes by the paw, not up on the leg! Animal rights people, the anti-trapping, anti-hunting fruitcakes who are constantly spewing lies and propaganda to the public, would have everyone believe that we use bear-sized traps that mangle animals' legs. They even produce fake, staged photos showing this. All of the traps they illustrate have sharp, steel teeth in the jaws. They speak of how many animals chew their feet and legs off to escape these super cruel devices. All of this is pure bull and lies. If you want to know the real truth and see for yourself, accompany a trapper on his trapline. The traps that we use today restrain coyotes, they don't torture them.

I often run across folks who have bought super large, dog-sized cage traps to catch coyotes in. Forget it—old wiley will rarely, if ever, be found caged up in one of these devices. It's a waste of both time and money. Call a good coyotero and he'll get the job done!

Using game calls to lure in coyotes to be shot is an old sport that has really grown in the number of participants in recent years. It is also a very effective method (at times) to use to control coyotes. Thousands of coyotes have been killed by predator callers while doing animal damage control. It has always been an important part of my work as a coyotero. I called in my first predator, a gray fox, over fifty years ago. Since that time, I've lured in several thousands of foxes, bobcats and coyotes with calls. For several years, I sold

*Expert coyote caller J.D. Piatt, Pro Staff Director for
Icotec Game calls has called coyotes over much of the U.S.*

my own brand of calls (Superior Predator Calls) and gave many
predator-calling seminars all across the country.

Often a coyotero can call in and kill a coyote or two that has
become wise to traps and snares. Coyotes can respond to calls in
daytime hours or night. They respond to daytime calling much
better in the western states. In the east, many successful coyote
killers are taking them at night using high-dollar night vision optics.
Calling coyotes successfully requires a bit of knowledge and good

Cierra Colvin with a coyote caught in a foot trap. She
also uses snares and predator calls to take coyotes.

equipment. It is also a sport that requires patience and persistence.

There are many brands and models of coyote-calling gear available today, and I will list reliable people whom you can purchase this gear from in another chapter. Anyone who owns a decent shotgun or rifle (.222 caliber or larger) can buy a ten-dollar mouth-blown predator call and kill coyotes if they learn the basics, hunt the right way and stick with it.

With coyote populations climbing in many parts of the U.S., more people have taken to running coyotes with dogs. This can be an effective way to control some coyotes. In the wide-open spaces in some parts of the Midwest and West, coursing hounds are often used. A mix of greyhounds and other dogs is used to run the coyotes down and bay them. A gritty "kill dog" or two in the pack will finish off the coyote. Coyotes are good runners, but they can't outrun the greyhounds or similar type dogs in the wide-open spaces.

In areas where there is more brush and woodlands, hounds are used to run coyotes. Some coyotes are caught by the hounds but most are shot running ahead of the hounds. Often other coyotes that are not being run by the hounds will pop out and the hunters may bag bonus coyotes. This is a growing sport in the east, and hounds are being selected and bred just for running coyotes.

Poisons of various kinds have killed untold numbers of coyotes. While the use of poisons is one of the most effective and easiest to use methods of coyote control, it is the most controversial. In many areas of the country the use of poisons is banned. Many of the professional coyoteros who have worked in the private and the government sector will tell you that poisons are a very valuable tool for controlling coyotes.

A shooter riding shotgun in a helicopter or airplane being used to flush coyotes from heavy cover has accounted for many dead coyotes. Aerial hunting of coyotes is limited, I believe, pretty much to the western parts of the country. It can be an effective method of controlling coyotes, but an expensive one.

Those of us who really see what's going on with coyotes across the country have come to believe that the government will never properly control coyotes, even if some who work there want to. There simply is just too much waste and politics and too many inefficient people working for government agencies for them to do a good job at controlling coyotes. Private contractors who are real, honest-to-God coyote killers are the only ones who can do this. Sportsmen, part-time trappers and hunters will help control populations, but they alone will never keep up with the growing populations. To make matter worse, the government bureaucrat academic types will continue to place more restrictions on those who do control coyotes effectively. Many seem to be obsessed with this.

I believe that the only way this trend can be reversed is by citizens, sportsmen and livestock producers putting pressure on legislators who are always hungry for more votes. It is a sad state of affairs, but we have seen that many of these people are not really concerned about the pros and cons of the issue itself; votes are what concerns them. But I do believe this is our only hope. Talking sense to the all-knowing, all-powerful bureaucrats and so-called wildlife managers has been, for the most part, a waste of time.

A good morning's catch on two small cattle farms.

A two-hole trap set for coyotes. Scent is placed in holes and trap is covered with dirt in front of holes.

This deer was killed by two bears. My wife and I were nearby and witnessed this. Coyotes ate what the bears left. Learning about what killed what is a part of studying coyotes.

CHAPTER 13

Do Your Own Coyote Studies

PEOPLE OFTEN QUESTION ME if they have coyotes on their place. While coyotes are widespread over all of North America and subject to pop up most anywhere, I can't truthfully answer them until I investigate their property or talk to another knowledgeable person who has seen evidence of coyotes on this particular property. For those of you who are interested in coyotes, I would suggest that you do some studies of your own. These efforts need not be complicated, nor do you need any academic training to conduct them. What you, yourself, learn on your own by actually studying the coyote in his element can be far more enlightening and meaningful than what you get out of a book, the computer or a video.

I believe that many people become aware of coyotes frequenting the vicinity by hearing their howls and vocalizations. Even people who have never heard the strange yipping, yapping and howling of coyotes often know what they are hearing for the first time. Their vocalizations are generally much different from their domesticated dog cousins. While many dogs, especially those in confinement, will howl when they hear a siren, the yips and howls of several coyotes responding to a siren are quite different. Once you hear them, you'll know what I'm speaking of.

Coyote vocalizations are very often heard just after darkness settles in and the coyotes start hunting. Various sounds are often made to locate other members of their group or to alert them to findings of food they have stumbled upon. Sometimes a few short and gruff barks are made to alert other coyotes in the area of impending danger. Single, unattached males will give out locater or lonesome howls to attract a female partner during the mating season. Coyotes can and will make any or all of these vocalizations anytime during the day or night when something prompts them to do so.

I purchased a small, handheld siren that runs off double A batteries from Southeastern Outdoor Supplies that can sometimes be played and cause coyotes in the area to howl. Serious coyoteros have used sirens to locate coyotes for years. Mouth-blown, handheld coyote howlers are inexpensive, and with a little practice, most anyone can replicate some of the howls and other vocalizations of coyotes. Coyotes will often answer these man-made calls. Many coyoteros can howl with their own voices. I learned this from a great old coyotero, the late Willis Kent of Montana, many years ago.

Over the years, I believe I have had more coyotes answer or respond to my howls from a time period beginning just before dark until an hour or so after daylight. But I have had many answer my howls all throughout the daylight hours, especially in the vast areas of the west. Keep in mind also that just because a coyote does not respond to your howls (or siren calls), it doesn't mean that they are not in the area or that they never travel through this area. A coyote may be in a certain area today or tonight and not come back through for several days. Some coyotes will not answer your howls for reasons you will never know. Remember that real coyoteros are persistent folks who do not let failures of any kind cause them to quit or give up. They take these sorts of things in stride.

Learning how to identify coyote tracks and then looking for them is a very simple way to determine if coyotes are using or traveling through an area. I have seen a few tracks left by mostly mixed-breed dogs with small feet that closely resembled coyote tracks. But

This is the front foot of a coyote. The length is always greater than the width.

in most cases, a coyote's foot will be more narrow than a dog's foot. Even a beagle's foot will be wider than the average coyote's foot. Also, when walking, a coyote and a fox will place one foot more directly in front of the other. The tracks will be in an almost straight line, while the dog tracks will be more scattered to the left or right.

Look for their tracks along farm and ranch roads, logging roads, cow and sheep paths, stock pens, sandwashes, plowed fields and water tanks. Check for tracks after rains, or look for them in the dust or sandy areas when the ground is hard and dry. Often, I have

A fresh pile of coyote poop. Note the persimmon seeds in it.

seen coyote tracks along the edge of mudholes in dirt roads where they stopped to lap up water. You may find coyote tracks along sandy beaches and sandbars found along streams. I have observed tracks in bare ground areas and in road ditches near subdivisions, shopping malls and athletic fields. After many years of controlling and studying coyotes, it doesn't surprise me to see their tracks anywhere. Hell, there may be coyote tracks on the moon!

Droppings or scat left by coyotes is another tell-tale sign of them passing through an area. Typical coyote droppings resemble those left by a domestic dog. Upon closer observation, you will see that coyote droppings will most always contain a mix of any and everything—hair or fur, bones, berry and fruit seeds, feathers and insects. Occasionally you will find deer hair and persimmon seeds in a dog's feces, but unless it was left by a feral or wild dog, you will also be able to see where the animal has eaten regular dog food.

Coyotes are famous for taking a crap right in the middle of a roadway. Often, I have seen where they backed up to a rock on the side of a road or along the edge of a field or hedgerow and let go. Bobcats will do the same. Why they like to do this, I don't know. I have most often avoided coyote control work in cities and urban areas because I do not care for hassles involved with such work, but on the few occasions when I have done this work, I have found coyote scat on paved streets, parking lots and sidewalks. When coyotes are feeding heavily on dead livestock and deer, elk, etc., you will usually see their droppings scattered around the carcass.

Actual coyote sightings are often rare for the average person under normal conditions. But where coyotes become overpopulated and in areas where they live and feed in close proximity to people, sightings are not as unusual. Since they do most of their traveling and hunting under the cover of darkness, they have fewer chances of being spotted. Many photos of coyotes pop up on wildlife cameras put out by hunters and wildlife enthusiasts who never knew that they were in the area. I often use these cameras in my coyote studies. Set them in the same places you look for tracks and around carcasses.

In areas where the ground surface is covered by grasses, leaves, etc. and coyotes leave no tracks, you can install "scent stations." To make a scent station, clear off an area about three feet in diameter and sift fine soil over the area. Have it smooth and even. You can dig up the soil and sift it back in or haul in sifted soil in five gallon (clean) buckets. In the center of this area, a scent or lure that will attract coyotes is placed on the end of a small stick or Q-tip and set sticking an inch or two out of the ground. When a coyote or other animals come to investigate the alluring odor, they will leave footprints in the soil for you to see. You can install sifted dirt patterns beside a rock, low stump or big clump of grass alongside the travelways and give the backing (rock, stump, grass) a shot of coyote urine. These dirt patterns need only be about 18" x 18", centered in front of the backing. Coyote urine and scents (lures) can be purchased from supply dealers that I have listed in another chapter.

For many years, those who formulate and sell scents and lures to trappers have utilized these scent stations to see how well the target animal responded to a certain smell. Wildlife researchers began using the scent stations when attempting to determine coyote populations. These stations will verify that coyotes use the area, but they cannot really determine how many. If your dirt pattern is full of coyote tracks, how can you determine how many left the tracks? You can't. It could have been one coyote or it could have been three. If another scent station a mile down the road shows coyote tracks, were they left by the same coyote or others? What if a coyote or several coyotes passed by the scent stations and didn't investigate the smell (for whatever reason)—can you honestly say there are no coyotes using the area?

I'll get to the point of this. Regardless of who conducts most coyote studies, be it "scientific" or "anecdotal," none of us can give highly accurate numbers regarding coyote populations. We can only give our best guess! What I have just written will anger some of the academics, but I could care less. We all are searching for truth and facts, aren't we? In many states, game department officials gather data on how many coyotes were shot or trapped, which is good. But the numbers they get in no way come close to the real numbers of coyotes actually killed. None of us will ever know how many were killed because so many kills are never reported. It's the same with reports that record livestock loss numbers due to coyotes. We may know how many were reported, but have no idea of how many were lost to coyote depredation. I know from personal experience that many livestock producers have no idea of the number of animals they have lost to coyotes. I caution you to be skeptical of many of the reports put out on coyotes by government officials and academics.

I encourage anyone, whether it is your desire to kill coyotes or not, to become a student of the coyote. It is a fascinating study indeed. What you see and learn on your own, in the field, you can believe.

Look for coyotes in areas where deer are having fawns.

Russ Carman, all around top trapper, lure
maker and author, a trapping legend.

CHAPTER 14

Can Coyotes Think?

I ONCE WATCHED TWO COYOTES as they came out of a pine thicket that bordered a cow pasture and attacked a big cow that had recently dropped a calf. One coyote kept rushing at the cow's head and the other one kept nipping at her hind legs. Fighting off the coyotes, the cow was soon away from her calf a few yards.

Coyote number three then appeared on the scene, grabbed the poor calf by the neck and quickly pulled it under a gate, out of the pasture. Tossing my binoculars into the truck seat, I hauled freight across the bumpy field in an effort to save the calf. I knew that the two coyotes badgering the mama cow wouldn't cause her any real harm and I could see the rest of the herd thundering across the pasture to come to her aid. Saving the calf was priority number one.

Halfway across the field I slid the truck to a stop, jumped out with my .243 and let go a round at the coyote that was mauling the calf. I missed and all three coyotes slid back under the fence and vanished into the pine woods. I arrived on the scene just as the bull and the rest of the herd reached the cow. The calf breathed its last breaths and died. I pushed the dead calf back under the gate where the mama could smell, lick and mourn over her loss. I had just witnessed an act of savagery and survival that plays out many times a day across America.

This incident and quite a few others that I have witnessed in my forty-plus years dealing with coyotes has caused me to believe that coyotes, at least some of them, can think to some degree! When I have brought this subject up around wildlife scientists, they laugh and argue that no animal can actually think. They will say that animal actions are for the most part instinctive. Some will admit that some animals can learn from events they experience. Well, how can any person or animal learn if they can't, to some degree, think? One of the definitions of "instinct" is "an action or reaction that is not learned."

I cannot believe that these three coyotes performed this act of killing through instinct alone. They knew better than to try and grab a calf that was surrounded by the herd. They had to go after one that was quite some distance away from others. The third coyote, the one that killed the calf, knew that the calf should be dragged out of the pasture where mama and the others could not get to them.

Let's look at another truth. No person, scientist or otherwise, has ever been able to put themselves into a coyote's body and see things as a coyote does using his brain and eyes! "Well, we've studied the brains of coyotes and other animals and have determined that they do not have the ability to think or reason," they tell us. They are telling us in a roundabout way that they (the scientists) are up there on the same level as God! It baffles me that there are so many gullible, non-thinking people in this world who believe most anything a scientist will say! If you take the time to read and evaluate many of the scientific studies that have been done on coyotes and other animals, you will begin to question their "truths" and "theories."

I have learned from wildlife scientists, biology professors and other academics. It is not my intent to badmouth them or portray any of them as being ignorant or less than good people. It is my intent, however, to hopefully make them aware of the fact that neither they nor myself have all the cut-and-dried answers. Learning is a process that never ends unless we close our minds to it and stop seeking the truth.

•••

Major Boddicker grew up on an Iowa farm and has trapped for 66 years: barn rats through coyotes, mice through leopards. He has a B.S. in biology, an M.S. in zoology, and a PH.D. in entomology. He studied wildlife for all of those degrees: rabbits, grouse, big game, and furbearers. He was an Extension Wildlife Specialist in Wildlife Damage Control and Furbearer Management at Colorado State University, Department of Fish and Wildlife Biology, from 1975 to 1984, and has done professional wildlife consulting from 1985 to the present. He was active in the USDA-sponsored coyote research committee (WRCC-26) from 1975-84, the golden age of coyote and predator research.

Dr. Major Boddicker, expert coyote killer, author, researcher and the maker of fine predator calls with a Colorado coyote.

Do Coyotes Think? by Major Boddicker

The time was the second week of June 1995. I was out looking for
coyote dens with a spotting scope from a distance of about a mile
when I spotted seven, which were bedded in the corner of an iso-
late CRP field on the Pawnee Grasslands, in eastern Colorado. The
wind was blowing at about five mph from the SSW, as usual.

About three-quarters mile to the northeast of the coyotes were
five antelope does with two, two-week-old fawns, loafing out in the
open short grass prairie about one-half mile from a north-south
four barbed wire fence.

Two of the coyotes got up, dropped down into a ravine, ran
down the ravine out of sight of the antelope and me, then up the
fenceline and crouched down behind the yucca plants near the antelope crawl under. When they were in place, the trap was set. From
the bedded coyotes to the fence was about one-and-a-half miles.

The other five coyotes got up, and in full view of the antelope,
slowly started hazing the antelope in a U-shaped line toward the
ambush. Always slowly, always acting like they were mousing and
not paying attention to the antelope, they moved closer but never
directly at the antelope.

The antelope, always looking back at the coyote line, slowly
and gradually moved toward the yuccas and fence crawl-under. It
took 45 minutes or more for the antelope to get to the fence crawl-
under.

The two coyote assassins were well-hidden in the yuccas, with
their scent blowing away from the unsuspecting antelope. The three
fawnless does ducked under the fence first with the does and fawns
at the end. The does with fawns ducked under, and as they did, the
coyotes struck, nailing the antelope fawns, latching on to the necks
and faces, bending and shaking them violently. The does, realizing

what happened, turned and tried to duck back under the fence to defend their fawns, only to be meet with five hazer coyotes that had arrived on a dead run to back up the assassins. The hazers blocked the does at the fence.

The does, realizing what had happened, ran off, stopped, and stood helplessly, stomping their feet and snorting, watching the coyotes kill the fawns and start eating them.

How in the world did the coyotes pull that off? If that was an example of non-thinking instinct, then how is thinking and planning defined?

Generally, many people dismiss the idea that anything but humans can think. We more earthy trappers and hunters tend to disagree. Why? Because we have personally witnessed actions by several species of wildlife that are very complicated, requiring forethought and planning. These behaviors are too complex to be simple instinct. One might assume that what we are dealing with is a question of semantics or word games, trying to draw a line between what is thinking and what is instinct-patterned behavior. I do not know where that line is.

I believe coyotes, beaver, and to a lesser degree foxes, wolves, raccoons, and bears possess higher levels of behavior that fit the thinking definition. Coyotes get up to hunt with a plan of where they are going and what they are going to do and somehow communicate to their packmates who is going to do what and when and how they will do it. To me, that requires thinking and is far beyond instinctive behavior alone.

Those of us who have done contract coyote and other pest control often face situations that are incredibly complicated. To do what coyotes do requires memory, consideration, planning, communication, and other mental processes that are not instinctual.

In Cherry Hills Village, Denver metro, in 1993, two coyotes set up an ambush on a city dog that included lying up against a house, one on each side of a sliding patio door. The coyotes had to jump a six-foot privacy fence to get to the yard and house.

At a precise time, 7:00 a.m. each day, the homeowner opened the sliding door to let out Fifi to do his morning pee. Bam! The coyotes instantly struck the dog at its first leap, one at the head and one over the kidneys. In an instant, the dog was dead. One coyote let go of the little dog; the other jumped the fence with the dog, followed by the other coyote. They ran, carrying the dog to a row of small pines that screened a swimming pool from the neighbors. They ate the dog by the swimming pool while the neighbors watched as they ate their breakfast.

How did those coyotes know the dog was going to be there? How did they know and remember what time it would be coming out to pee? Which coyote would grab which end of the dog? Which one would carry off the dog? How did they know what time to get in place on each side of the door? Happenstance? Instinct? No, there has to be more to a coyote's brain and ability than that.

When coyotes are setting up and executing these fairly complicated plans, how do they decide which one is the boss? How do they communicate that and the plans to each other? Which of them makes the necessary observations they need prior to the ambush to plan the ambush?

In our inadequate way, humans tend to believe we stand apart with unique abilities as God's sole identified and favored thinking creations: we are apart and above everything else. I am not so sure. I think it is smarter to be a hunter and trapper as part of the pack. It seems more plausible to me that God's plan has been more of an interrelated continuum. As we creatures have been created in God's long and slow evolutionary process, many varieties of mental capacities have developed. Since life began, we end products of several billion years of evolution all share half of chemically identical DNA. Why would we not share at some level a brain function we call thinking? Why don't we compromise and come up with an intermediate category that allows for both instinct and thinking to describe complex animal behaviors? That way we can understand and communicate how teenagers, urban liberals, North Koreans, and possums make it in this world.

May I speculate that not only coyotes can think at complex levels, they communicate by a very complex language that includes making and sensing both sub- and ultra-sonic sound waves above and below the spectrum, which humans can't hear. They can also communicate with at least an equal variety of scents and visual posturing in their facial expressions and body and hair movements that we can see but do not know what they mean.

On a scale of 0 being the dumbest living thing and 10 being the smartest human, where would I put a coyote? I'd put the smartest of them between 4.5 and 5.5. Of course, at being the creature they evolved to be, they are a 10.

The smart ones I have to trap, which are pestering people, are such intelligent thinkers that I name them out of awed respect. An urban ARF is easier to catch.

One becomes accomplished at beating coyotes when one can think like a coyote.

Do coyotes reason? Contemplate? Dream? Do they have complex and recoverable memories? Do they show affection, sorrow and remorse? These are conversations for another day.

••••

Oscar Cronk of Maine is one of the most well-known and respected trappers to ever lace up a pair of boots and go to the wilderness. He is also known for his ability to make trapping and dog-training scents that are some of the best. Oscar also gleaned all of the information he could from some of the old-time great trappers,

Legendary trapper, woodsman, bobcat hunter and lure maker Oscar Cronk of Maine pulling out a beaver from under the ice. This man has decades of experience with northern brushwolves.

hunters and houndsmen whom he admired. Even though the years have piled up on him, his eyes still have a sparkle to them and he still traps and hunts in the Maine wilderness. When Oscar Cronk speaks, it pays to shut up and listen.

Thoughts On Animal Behavior by Oscar Cronk

As a trapper, hunter, and trailing dog trainer, I have studied animal habits and behavior for over 70 years. I have come to this conclusion: some animals are smarter than others. After studying animals under all conditions, I find the best teachers are the animals themselves. I agree with most people that animals operate mostly on instinct; however, I have experienced many times where wild animals as well as domestic animals used reasoning to solve a problem.

I have caught hundreds of mink during my trapping career, but one old battle-scared male seemed to show more than instinct. He refused to go near the stream's edge, staying entirely on the bank. He left his calling card, a huge set of droppings on a moss-covered log. I studied the log and decided how he would jump down or up on the log, depending if he was coming up or down the stream. I bedded a clean waxed no. 2 fox trap with five feet of chain and grapple in a scooped-out depression and added guide and stepping sticks. His jump landed him square on the pan and he jumped for the water. Upon examination I found he had lost toes on three of his feet. He avoided all water sets and, apparently, his forages on land kept him fat and healthy.

I once had a male blue tick bobcat hound, probably one of the best I ever owned. Once every few years when tracks were slow in coming he would jump a deer. One night I saw him jump a deer and he ran it tight and hot on the trail. I hollered and fired my pistol and he quit running the track. After several minutes I heard him tree barking but not with his usual vigor. Upon investigation, I found him treeing on a porcupine. He had never run or tree barked on a porcupine before or afterwards. He figured he could fool me and I wouldn't know he had run a deer.

I have seen tracks of mink, raccoon, bobcat, fox and coyote on snow react beyond their natural instincts. To notice this one must slow down and consider what animals are really doing.

My old friend, Fred Goodwin, who hunted and trapped for over 80 years and died at the age of 102, had many interesting stories of unusual animal behavior. His favorite was how he finally bagged the legendary Silver Ridge buck. The old buck always traveled with a barren doe. The buck would wait until the doe came out and checked the surrounding; if anything was amiss she wouldn't make the call to him. The morning Fred shot the old monarch the doe appeared and was nervous. Fred moved not a muscle, scarcely breathing. Finally, she settled and made the call. Within five minutes he came out. A well-placed shot dropped the old veteran that Fred had hunted for four years.

I will always believe that some animals, like people, are smarter than others and can reason beyond their natural instincts.

••••

Mike Marsyada of Pennsylvania is another well-known, well-respected trapper, hunter and lure, scent and bait maker who has spent his life in the trapping field. His books on trapping are considered to be classics by many. Mike's dealing with coyotes have taken him to other states, and he has been a student of the wiley coyote for a long time. When Mike tells you something, you can go to the bank with it!

Can Coyotes Think by Mike Marsyada

While I am not one of those folks who would attribute super human abilities to the coyote and his kind, I have been at this game for long enough to have seen him do some things which one can only logically conclude had to be achieved after some amount of reasoning on the part of the coyote. Simply passing off some of these experiences as the product of instinct would be serious short-changing of the coyote's ability to think.

Admittedly some coyotes are no harder to catch than the average possum, but there are more than a few that are, at least in some small part, responsible for some of the lack of hair on my head and the white whiskers on my face.

On more than one occasion I have seen in the snow where a pack of coyotes would drive deer into an ambush and use the wind

Mike Marsyada, life-long trapper, lure maker and student of wildlife with some winter caught coyotes.

in their favor to do it. I have also, on more occasions than I care to admit, been forced to snare a problem coyote, simply because he would not commit to work any of my best attempts to catch him in a steel trap.

There was a reason the native American Indian held him in such reverence, and the older I get, the easier it is for me to understand why....

••••

Wayne Derrick is a New Mexico trapper who has put in a lot of years killing stock-killing coyotes. He has also made his living at times as a fur trapper. While working as a coyote man for the U.S.D.A., he racked up thousands of coyote kills. Wayne also had the opportunity to learn from some of the old-time coyoteros who knew coyotes in and out. Wayne is a true coyotero and I'm proud to call him friend.

Can Coyotes Think by Wayne Derrick

Over the years, I have witnessed how a lot has changed in regards to the coyote, methods used to control them and how trappers and others view the coyote. Much of my life has been spent in the wilds studying and controlling coyotes. I was blessed by the fact that along with my own experiences, I had the opportunity to learn more from some of the best coyote men that ever lived. These men killed thousands of coyotes using all sorts of methods: poisoning (1080, strychnine, M44's), helicopters and airplanes, steel traps, snares, calling, denning, ambushing and by making coyote drives on foot, horseback, dirtbikes, ATVs and vehicles.

Like myself, these men were of the "old school" way of thinking and they had common sense. They devoted their lives to controlling coyotes and knew more about coyotes than most any of the trappers, hunters and wildlife managers of today. They were honest, hardworking, solid men and I don't think any of them could have been accused of being "politically correct." One of the big changes I have seen is that of many trappers, wildlife officials and others not having a good, complete knowledge of coyotes. There is a lot of false information out there these days and some information that is partly or all true, but not complete. I'm not trying to be negative or pick on anyone, but there are some out there who don't know what they think they know.

I don't believe that coyotes will ever build an automobile or fly an airplane, but to say that they can't think to some degree is wrong. Many dollars have been spent to either eliminate all coyotes from the face of the earth or to control them, but their numbers increase all over the country, especially when there is little control work being done. If coyotes couldn't think and learn somewhat, they would have vanished like the wolves.

A friend of mine who was raised on a large sheep ranch and ramrodded several others told me of an interesting encounter he had with coyotes. He was waiting in a sheep pasture for some horsebackers to come his way gathering sheep when he saw a female coyote with three pups leave the open pasture and disappear into a jag of woods and brush. He smiled and thought that when his helpers came they would surround the coyotes, flush them out and get all of them. They had been losing sheep and he'd bet that this female was doing the killing.

While he was waiting, the female coyote came out of cover to a fence and climbed over it. She could have jumped the fence or she could have gone under it. Well, the sheepman thought, she might get away but we'll get the pups. But then the pups came out and also climbed over the fence just as she had done! It dawned on the man that this coyote knew a thing or two about fences and danger.

Apparently she had seen other coyotes get hung in snares that crawled under fences. She knew that the pups couldn't jump the fence, so the old gal had shown them how to climb over the fence. When this female sensed impending danger and knew that she had to get her pups safely out of this pasture, some light must have come on in her head and she got them to safety or they all could have died. Somewhere during this episode a simple thought process must have occurred. I don't see how anyone could say that her actions were 100% instinctive.

Many times, I have found where coyotes have moved a fence snare out of the way to safely enter a pasture to kill or cross through to go somewhere else. Now once in a while a coyote could get lucky and move or knock a snare out of position, but when one does this continuously, I get worried. I have to change my tactics to catch it. I know I'm dealing with a coyote that can think.

I've watched and seen where coyotes tried to dig up a stake that was holding the trap they were in. Did they know that I had put the stake in? No, I don't think so. That would have been giving them too much credit. But did they think (and know) that the trap stake was holding them there? Yes.

Can some coyotes reason? Yes. Can some coyotes think? Yes.

••••

Russ Carman is well known throughout the trapping community and for many years has been one of the top lure-making guys in North America. His opinion on whether coyotes can think or not differs somewhat from mine, but I have a lot of respect for him and what he has learned over a period of many years.

Can Coyotes Think by Russ Carman

Can coyotes think? It's a question I doubt anyone can answer with certainty. But as a person who has tinkered with the making of lures for the last 60 years I have always worked on the assumption that animals are overwhelmingly influenced by their instincts. At the same time I'm fully aware of the fact that coyotes, like dogs, have an amazing capacity to learn. Now, do they put into use what they've learned through the power of thought, or thinking, or does that acquired knowledge simply sharpen and expand their instinctive reactions? I believe it's the latter. For example: If a coyote's mate is caught in a trap at a set that reeks of the smell of a certain lure, will he fear and avoid every set where he smells that same odor based on his ability to use reason and logical thought? (A fear based on what he's learned by prior experience.) I think the answer is no.

Instinctive reactions, both good and bad, as illustrated above, are caused by outside stimuli. Even a small dog trained to make a back flip will never execute that move without first receiving a command to do so—a knowledge acquired and maintained by the reward he receives for doing it. The command, in this example, becomes the outside stimuli.

Animals naturally fear certain things, and they can learn to fear certain other things, but their reaction to those things they fear is always instinctive, and I believe the same applies to most everything they do. But I do believe that some coyotes, to some degree, can think. If they couldn't, there wouldn't be many coyotes left!

••••

So can coyotes think? Yes, to some extent I believe some can. Others who have spent lifetimes controlling and studying coyotes in the field tend to agree with me. Are we all wrong and are the college boys right? I'll let you decide on that. By the way, two of the coyotes involved in the calf killing incident that I shared with you at the beginning of this chapter wound up in traps that I sat near the calf carcass. Other coyotes on the same farm died within the same week.

Much of what we hear about controlling coyotes is pure hogwash. This old boy killed a bunch of sheep and lambs.

CHAPTER 15

The 70% Theory
Is Coyote Population Control Possible?

by Gerry Lavigne

AUTHORS NOTE: Gerry Lavigne is a widely known and well-respected wildlife biologist who resides in the state of Maine. With an academic background in wildlife management and with years of field experience as a coyote hunter, Gerry has learned a lot about coyotes. He uses scientific data, field observations, study and common sense to form his ideas and opinions on coyotes. The following article written by Gerry appeared in *Trapper's Post* magazine. Following Gerry's article, there is a response to it written by Major Boddicker, a Colorado coyotero who has contributed to this book in the *Can Coyotes Think?* chapter. I am mighty glad that there are at least a few men such as Gerry and Major who are not afraid to disagree with other academics and government wildlife agency folks.

••••

IN THE CASE OF THE 70% ESTIMATE, the scientific method ran off the tracks. I have searched the scientific literature extensively, yet I have been unable to find *any* scientific studies conducted in the last 40 years that sought to test the accuracy and truth of this 70% model.

No question, coyotes are controversial. And nothing about them is more controversial than whether we can control their numbers. When allowed to live at their biological maximum population size, coyotes often conflict with man, as hungry coyotes prey extensively on deer, turkeys, small game, livestock and pets. Understandably, we would like to manage coyote populations at lower numbers to alleviate some of these predatory problems. But is this possible?

For a very long time now, wildlife biologists have told us that coyote population control would be difficult or impossible. They quote a statistic that says we would need to remove 70% of the coyote population every year to cause a population decline. Anything less than that supposedly allows the coyote's alleged extraordinary reproductive potential to replace those killed. Some biologists (usually those sympathetic to the anti-hunting and anti-trapping movement) even go so far as to predict that any attempt to reduce coyotes will cause their numbers to *increase* above original population levels, as reproduction kicks into high gear.

Is all this true? It must be, if scientists say so, right?

I think I smell a rat!

Those same biologists who claim coyotes cannot be controlled also caution us not to kill too many gray wolves. Wolves must be spared the ravages of hunting and trapping, or their precarious populations will dwindle to extinction. But how can two wild canines, with very similar reproductive traits and social organization, be so different in their response to man-caused mortality? Both mate for life; both live in family groups or packs; both produce one similar-sized litter annually. There are some differences between coyotes and wolves in this regard, but these will be spelled out later.

If it's impossible to control coyotes without removing at least 70% of them, why is removing even a few wolves supposedly a threat to their numbers? You can't have it both ways.

The coyote is a true survivor and can adapt to live most anywhere.

Where did that infamous 70% mortality figure for coyotes come from?

It originated from a population "model" that was published at a conference in the mid-1970s. Like all models, it was pieced together as a "best guess" estimate of how coyotes in the western US would react to intensive hunting and trapping pressure. And like all models, that prediction (i.e. 70% mortality) is only as accurate as the reliability of its component parts.

In science, a model (or a hypothesis) is just a *starting* point toward understanding what the model is trying to predict. After constructing the model, scientists then design experiments or field studies to test its accuracy. New results allow refinement of the model, which leads to further studies. This is the scientific method. It is both job security for scientists and a necessary step toward advancing knowledge. Especially in wildlife biology, there is no such thing as "settled science," because there are too many changing variables in the environment for one model to behave the same in every place, at every time, and at every population level.

In the case of the 70% estimate, the scientific method ran off the tracks. I have searched the scientific literature extensively, yet I have been unable to find *any* scientific studies conducted in the last 40 years that sought to test the accuracy and truth of this 70% model. Rather, I have observed almost universal acceptance of it among wildlife biologists. As a result, the 70% estimate is now treated as an immutable law. It has been parroted by countless biologists (myself included in the past)—even though most of these biologists probably have never read the report or know where it originated. I find this to be somewhat shameful and a blemish on the credibility of the wildlife profession.

Worse, the anti-hunting crowd treats the 70% estimate as something akin to the laws of physics, which are set in stone. The estimate is just too convenient for them to quote as supposed "proof" that it is useless to trap or hunt coyotes to solve predation problems, since all it does is create more coyotes. It very nicely fits the agenda of the anti crowd—and of many biologists who have a tendency to want nature to function apart from the hand of man.

For once, let's take a look at the underpinnings of this model.

The extraordinarily high reproductive rate predicted for western coyotes depends on three related factors: 1) age at first reproduction, 2) compensatory reproduction, and 3) compensatory mortality.

The 70% model assumes that once you start whittling down the population, *all* age classes of females will subsequently become pregnant. This includes young-of-the-year (juvenile) coyotes, which would be only about 10 months of age when first mated. These youngsters are always the most numerous age class in the population, and the 70% model really expects them to become pregnant in high numbers. This becomes even more important after control efforts continue year after year, because the number of older, mature coyotes dramatically declines.

The second factor, compensatory reproduction, predicts that the number of pups in the average litter will increase in the face of predator control on coyotes. The logic is simple. When you remove a good many coyotes, there is more food available for the survivors. Improved nutrition among mated females would lead to larger litters.

The third factor, compensatory mortality, assumes that as hunting and trapping activity increases, coyote losses to *natural* mortality will decrease, or be eliminated entirely. This theory holds that the (temporarily) smaller coyote population, being better fed, will incur fewer losses to pup malnutrition, infectious diseases, predation by other coyotes or other predators, etc. Therefore, in order to reduce coyote numbers in the face of diminishing natural losses, hunting and trapping must pick up the slack, to the tune of 70% annual removal of the population.

As mentioned, little has been done to test the accuracy of these three factors among western coyotes. But that is not even relevant for those of us in climates with deep snows. Eastern coyotes are a good example. They are a bit different than their western counterparts, as a result of interbreeding with wolves on their way over here. Eastern coyotes exhibit some wolf-like traits, including delayed dispersal, greater tendency to hunt in packs through winter, a predilection for larger prey like deer (made possible by larger body size and weight), and finally, delayed reproduction.

The Eastern coyote has received some basic research that can be used to evaluate the 70% model. First, you cannot rely on the youngest coyotes to get pregnant as the population is reduced. Like wolves, most Eastern coyotes apparently are first bred in their second year, *if* then. Reproduction is a biological luxury among wild animals. It is possible only after body growth, and body maintenance requirements, are met. Female pups generally cannot put on enough weight and fat to go into heat in mid-winter, given the limited food resources typically available during late fall and early winter near the northern limit of their range.

It is likely that reduction of pack size by trapping and hunting of these coyotes during fall and early winter will further diminish the number of pup female coyotes that can go into heat by February. Predation efficiency and success increases with pack size. Hence, breaking down pack cohesion and size would work against hunting success, as snows deepen and prey becomes harder to find and kill.

Whether in the East or elsewhere, the concept of compensatory reproduction has some flaws. Both litter size and survival of the pups are higher among mature coyotes than among young breeders. Mature breeders, having completed body growth, have more energy to apply toward reproduction. In addition, the experience gained from past pregnancies helps improve survival tactics once pups are born. Intense hunting and trapping removes many of these experienced breeders, leaving a higher proportion of young coyotes to pick up the slack. And in snowy climates, young coyotes have enough trouble surviving to spring, let alone becoming burdened with litters of eight or more pups. Don't count on compensatory reproduction to bolster coyote population growth in these winter conditions!

The same goes for compensatory mortality. The 70% western coyote model assumed that coyote control work was happening at the same time of year that most natural mortality would occur. That's not true here. Most natural losses, among young coyotes at least, occur during spring into early autumn. Most hunting and trapping mortality here in the East occurs during fall and winter. Rather than cancelling each other out, a good portion of man-caused mortality *adds* to whatever amount of natural losses have already occurred. Studies in Maine indicate that natural mortality among Eastern coyotes amounts to 20% to 25% of the population annually—before we even set the first trap!

The bottom line is this: Eastern coyotes are prolific enough, but they *can* be managed. Their all-cause highest mortality rate to control them is more like 50% (as it is with wolves), rather than the 70% predicted (but untested) model for western coyotes. And with 20% to 25% mortality going to natural causes, reaching that control mortality of 50% only requires that trapping and hunting kick in an additional 25% to 30% of the annual population.

This is doable, and in fact it is being done, on a small to regional scale around Maine at this time. During recent years we have observed *lower* coyote abundance in several areas for a year or two following intensive removals by dog hunting, or intensive trapping and shooting. We have documented a collapse in reproductive activity, due to social chaos brought about by three years of intensive dogging and bait hunting over a five-town area in the mid-coast of Maine. We have documented coyote removals amounting to 30% of the fall population resulting from a coyote hunting contest conducted over a 600-square mile area.

It is shameful that state and university biologists have no interest in scientifically testing the 70% coyote control model as it applies to the Eastern coyote. Field testing these elements of coyote control has been repeatedly recommended by sportsmen (and yours truly) since at least the mid-1980s, all to no avail. For now, we will have to be content with watching our biologists foolishly parrot an untested model, and dress it up as "settled science."

Outdoorsmen, on the other hand, should continue to refine their hunting and trapping techniques, protect their existing hunting and trapping opportunities, and grow the sport of coyote hunting. And by default, we may well prove the parrots wrong about coyote control in winter climate areas.

••••

Major Boddicker, PhD, is a world-reknown wildlife researcher and scientist and has been a student of coyotes for many years. He not only has academic creditials, he has worked in the field controlling coyotes for a very long time. Here's his reply to Lavigne's article.

GREAT ISSUE of *Trapper's Post*! As I read Gerry Lavigne's article, "The 70% Solution: Is Coyote Control Possible?" I have had those same thoughts, experienced the same observations, and had the same doubts about the infamous 70% magical model—since I first heard the report 40 years ago. I was working at Colorado State University at the time the report was first published. I was working with coyotes, choosing to do *lethal* control research, not the *nonlethal* control that was getting all the research money.

The authors of that 70% study were and are acquaintances of mine; they are pro-coyote management, and solid guys. They have been surprised also at the weight that study has been given. Several of them expressed doubts about it shortly after, and since. It was *not* an end-all fact on which to base 40 years of predator management strategy; it was not intended to be.

The 70% study gave the coyote lovers and anti managers a theoretical anchor on which to push forward their theories that coyote population control is too expensive, and an exercise in futility. I disagreed then, and I disagree now. Managed predation control is a solid positive.

Gerry Lavigne has summarized the continent-wide coyote population management situation concisely and accurately. Bravo! It's the best presentation I have read.

My guess is that the recent research on eastern coyotes would fit like a sock over the western coyote population parameters. After all, a significant portion of eastern coyote ancestors were hauled east from Wyoming, Texas, South Dakota, and Indiana over the past 40 years for the dog trial clubs.

I would describe the research done on western coyotes over the last 40 years as having a lack of focus, too narrow in scope, too short in duration, and set up with faulty inputs and disregard of important variables. Some were done with a predetermined outcome in mind. Some have been done by researchers who have been biased *against* any sort of lethal interventions.

Actual study outcomes on predation losses of big game and livestock have almost unanimously shown that coyote predation is a significant factor in reducing surpluses of mule deer, white-tailed deer, and antelope available for hunting. Sage hens, sharp-tails, and in some regions waterfowl, pheasants, and quail can be included in the species affected.

The state and federal wildlife agencies are quite aware of this. Why don't they do anything about it? Because it is contrary to their personal beliefs. And they want to spend the money on themselves rather than on long-term predator management programs, regardless of their potential benefits.

In my experience, without trappers and varmint hunters and the continuing popularity of both activities, in spite of low fur prices and harassment of fur dealers by state and federal law enforcement continent-wide, wildlife agencies would be even further in the hole and sliding faster down than they are. The millions of predators we trappers and hunters take out each fall have an enormous impact on keeping game populations on the positive side.

Trappers and varmint hunters pay for the privilege of losing millions of dollars in pursuit of their sports, which significantly benefits all of the other wildlife users. When was the last time trappers or varmint hunters have been given a public "Thank you" by state or federal wildlife agencies, or the Elk Foundation, Ducks

Unlimited, Wild Turkey Federation, or any others, for helping keep our wildlife in reasonable numbers?

I hope Gerry Lavigne continues to write on this general topic. I hope *Trapper's Post* readers read Gerry's work carefully, so they "get it."

Thanks, Gerry, for writing this, and thank you, Bob, for publishing it. —Major L. Boddicker

Snares set in pathways catch coyotes.

*My friend Tim holding a city coyote caught
in a field between two subdivisions.*

Craig and Dana O'Gorman being honored at an event for their dedicated service to Powder River County, Montana, controlling coyotes. Craig is one of the best coyote men ever to set a trap or snare for coyotes. He gives on the line instructions for a fee that has produced some top coyote men.

CHAPTER 16

Learning How To Control Coyotes

I N A PREVIOUS CHAPTER I discussed methods of controlling coyotes. Learning the basics of setting a trap or a snare or how to use a predator call to kill a coyote are pretty simple, but there's much more to learn to be a successful taker of coyotes. The process of learning about coyotes and how to take them is a never-ending process for all of us, even the pros. The coyote's ability to survive under pressure has shown us that we will never eradicate all of them (and we shouldn't), and this has also shown us that we must constantly learn how to improve our skills in order just to keep their numbers under control.

The use of proper equipment when controlling coyotes is an absolute necessity. Yes, some coyotes are killed every year by lucky hunters or trappers who use substandard equipment and shoddy methods. These people will never put a dent in the coyote population, and they will most often educate coyotes to the point where even a real coyotero will have problems killing them. In this chapter I will discuss what is needed and even the brands of equipment that myself and other real coyote men use. When I mention a particular brand of anything, it is not intended to be a sales pitch; I am merely sharing what I and other experienced coyote takers use. What we use has stood the test of time, and it is what we use to get the job done in the correct way.

*Willis Kent (deceased) has just made a howl and he and his
coyote dog (Fuzz) are waiting for a reply. I learned so much
from this Montana coyotero and am truly thankful.*

I have been approached many times in my lifetime by people
who say they desire to become successful coyote hunters, trappers,
or both. When I explain to them what it will involve in both time
and money, most of them give up the idea. Some will not listen to
my advice and attempt to cut corners, but they never become good
coyote men. These "half-asser" types (as I call them) may take a
coyote or two, and many of them will lie and brag about their half-

assed successes. There will be people who will even believe these jokers, but real coyoteros will spot one of these guys a mile away. The proof will always be in the pudding! The number of competent coyote takers in this country is a low one.

The very best way to get a solid jump start on being a successful coyote taker is to go with a man who has a lot of experience and knows his business. You may learn a good bit by going with someone who calls, traps or snares 10 to 30 coyotes a year. But you will stand to learn more by going with a man who kills coyotes for a living. Even as a kid I always wanted to go with and be taught by the best, even if it was learning about trapping muskrats. As with many other endeavors we take on in life, shortcuts and half measures often lead to failure and disappointments.

If you are fortunate enough to learn from a pro coyotero for free, you are a lucky man. If you have to pay for instructions from a real pro, you are still well ahead of the game. A good coyote man can show and teach a student in one to three days (in the field) what might take him twenty years, on his own, to learn. The pro will not only show you how he sets a trap or hangs a snare, but why he did it. He can teach you much about coyotes, their habits, travel patterns, etc. that he has learned from a lifetime of experience. Much of what he can show and teach can never be gleaned from books and videos.

You can learn how to catch, call or kill coyotes by reading, watching videos and attending trapping seminars. Nearly every state in the U.S. and every province in Canada has a trapper's association that holds annual conventions and gives seminars on trapping. There will be dealers there also who sell trapping/hunting supplies. This information can be gotten off of the computer. Trapping conventions are the continuance of the old mountain man rendezvous of yesteryear, and there is often much to see at them. You also get to meet guys (and gals) who are experts at taking coyotes and other animals.

The key factor that determines whether or not you become a successful coyotero is that of wanting to be one bad enough. The equipment, help and assistance is out there if you are dedicated to going about it the right way and work hard at it. I can guarantee that you will encounter many frustrations as long as you chase coyotes; even the pros do at times. Persistence, the desire to succeed and the ability to solve problems that occur will be factors that determine how good a coyotero you'll be.

I will now list some of the products that myself and other coyoteros use in our everyday work, along with info on where you can buy them. I will also list books and videos that are good and will help you along the way. I am endorsing these products, people and firms. I have experience with them and they have stood the test of hard use and time. There are others out there that I don't use regularly that are good also. And yes, as with everything, there are a few ripoffs. It doesn't take anyone long to separate the wheat from the chaff if he stays up on his game. I am not much of computer person, but I hear that there is much to be found on various computer sites about coyotes and coyote control. I'm sure that some of this information is good, but I have seen a little that told me immediately that the person giving out information on coyotes didn't know much of anything about them or how to control them.

Good equipment is a must for coyote control work. These 3 foot traps are some of the best. On the left is the Minnesota Brand 550. Center is Graham's #2 and right is Graham's #3 Montana, Craig O'Gorman sells a modified coyote trap that is excellent.

Trapping & Snaring Supply Dealers

1 - Southeastern Outdoor Supplies, Inc.
    4250 Figsboro Road
    Martinsville, VA 24112
    (276) 638-4698

Southeastern is one of the largest and oldest trapping supply dealers in North America. You can go online or call them for a free current catalog. They also carry hunting supplies, dog supplies, archery equipment, clothing, boots, books, videos and muzzleloading supplies. They carry many brands of predator calls. This is a top-notch firm to deal with.

2 - O'Gorman Enterprises, Inc.
    P.O. Box 491
    Broadus, MT 59317
    (406) 436-2234

Craig and Dana O'Gorman have been in business for many years, producing lures, baits and other trapping supplies that are as good as money can buy. All of what they use and sell has undergone rigorous testing under harsh Montana conditions. They charge $7.00 for their huge catalog (refundable on your first order) that is well worth the price, and you will truly enjoy reading through it. Craig has made his living controlling coyotes and is considered to be one of the best coyoteros in the country.

3 - Renno's Animal Lures
    Juniata Valley Trapper Supply
    251 Maple Lane
    Mifflintown, PA 17059
    (717) 463-3624

Leroy Renno carries a good line of trapping supplies along with his lures. His handmade, wooden fur stretchers are tops and the heavy-duty trapper's trowel he sells is the best I've ever used. Send $2.00 for a catalog.

4 - Grawe's Lures & Trapping Supplies
    Box 306
    Wahpeton, ND 58074
    (218) 643-3292

Ardel Grawe has been in business for 45 years and has trapped and hunted much longer. All of Grawe's products are trapline tested. Write or call for his catalog. I rate Ardel as A#1!

5 - Sterling Fur Co.
  11268 Frick Rd.
  Sterling, OH 44276
  (303) 939-3763

This trapping supply dealer has been around for many years and carries a large selection of trapline tested gear. Send $1.00 for catalog. Good folks to deal with!

6 - Minnesota Trapline Products
  7444 County Road 27 NW
  Pennock, MN 562790
  (320) 599-4176

Tim and Nancy Caven (and kids) built a large, successful trapper's supply company from scratch. They stock anything a trapper could ever need and their Minnesota Brand Coyote traps are as good as any I've ever used. Call or write for a catalog.

7 - Snare One
  P.O. Box 378
  Port Republic, NJ 08241
  (609) 748-3541

Newt Sterling, the owner of Snare one, is widely respected as a top snare man throughout North America. He makes top quality snares and also sells a variety of trapping supplies. Newt is as good as they come! Call or write for a catalog.

8 - John Graham's Fur Country Lures
  P.O. Box 312
  Lusk, WY 82225
  (307) 334-9930

John Graham kills coyotes for a living in Wyoming. He uses the same lures and baits that he makes to sell on his own trapline. He developed and manufactures his own brand of coyote traps that are top quality and get the job done right. John is a for-real coyotero. Call or write for a catalog.

9 - Dakota Line
    108 North Main Street
    Lennox, S.D. 57039
    (605) 744-0133

The folks at Dakota Line specialize in snares but sell other products as well. Their products are built for trappers by real trappers. Write or call for catalog.

Trapping Lures, Scents & Baits

A wide variety of baits, lures and scents have been used for years to bring coyotes in to the trapper's traps or snares. I have caught hundreds on natural baits such as chunks of rabbit, deer, groundhog and bobcat meat. Whole, dead mice make good baits for old wiley. Trappers have been concocting smells to lure in coyotes for many centuries. Some of the lures and scents are made by using glands taken from coyotes, other use a mix of several different glands from several different animals. Some lures are made from exotic musks, and skunk musk attracts coyotes. Coyote, fox and bobcat urine will attract coyotes. A lot of study, experimenting and hard work goes into scent and lure making to produce the desired product.

The making of really effective coyote lures, scents and baits is an art in itself. There are some great scent makers, a bunch of so-sos and some who should give it up. I will now list the ones that I use the most, ones that I have taken a few thousands of coyotes with. This is not to say that there aren't other good products out there. Most of the supply dealers previously listed sell their own brand of good smells and some sell other brands as well.

1 - *Marsyada's Lures* –
Mike Marsyade probably knows as much about concocting lures as any man alive. His "Coyote Lure Supreme" and his "All Call" lure have aided me in catching a lot of coyotes. Most all of the large supply dealers carry his lures.

2 – *John Graham's Fur Country Lures* –
I've always caught coyotes on John's lures. His "Super Bonanza," "Deception" and "Seduction" lures have called in many coyotes for me. His "Bonanza Cold" lure has a goodly amount of skunk smell in it and is a great long distance call lure. Lasting, quality lures with a capital "Q."

3 – *O'Gorman's Lures* –
I have used Craig O'Gorman's coyote lures for years and have never been disappointed. They are top notch. His "Powder River Paste Bait" has called in hundreds of coyotes for me. I have used about all of his coyote lures with good success, but some of my favorites are "Coyote Gland," "Coyote Matrix" and "Long Distance Call."

4 – *Leroy Renno's Lures* –
Leroy makes two coyotes lures that have been good producers for me, "Magic Touch" and "Predator Man." Coyotes are sure to investigate these two smells.

5 – *Milligan Brand Lures* –
I've known Ray Milligan for many years and have used his "Steppenwolf I" and "Steppenwolf II" lures for about as long as he's made them. They've helped me put a lot of coyote hides on my fur stretchers. Many supply dealers carry Milligan Brand Lures or you can order them online at Ray@MilliganBrand.com.

6 – *Cronk's Lures* –
Legendary Maine trapper Oscar Cronk learned much about the art
of lure making from some of the old greats of trapping, McGowan,
Arnold and Lynch. His "Allagosh Fur Call," "Coyote Supreme" and
"Predator 500" have always produced coyotes for me. Many dealers
sell Oscar's lures.

7 – *Carman's Lures* –
    Pro Grade Lures
    415 Williams Pond Rd.
    New Milford, PA 18834
    (570) 278-1081
Another name that is a legend among trappers and lure makers.
Russ Carman deserves a PhD degree in lure making. His "Musk
Formula," "Vent Scent," "Pro's Choice" and "Final Touch" lures are
tops on coyotes. Most dealers carry his lures.

8 - *Grawe's Lures* –
Ardel Grawe has been trapping and making lures for a long time.
For coyotes I like his "Yote Duster," "Dakota Gland," and "K-7." His
"Prarie Fire Bait" is very good. You can't go wrong with Grawe's
lures and baits.

9 – Derrick's Lures
    P.O. Box 111
    Maljamar, NM 88264
    (575) 676-0001
Wayne Derrick has been trapping for over half a century, much of
this time being devoted to coyote control. I feel confident using any
of his lures.

10 - Rob Erickson
   On Target ADC
   P.O. Box 469
   Cortland, IL 60112
   (815) 286-3073

Rob Erickson studies and probably catches more city/urban coyotes than any other trapper I know of. You can depend on what he makes and sells to trappers.

Others

A young fellow by the name of Wilson, who makes Wilson's Sure Fire Lures, is sort of a new kid on the block in the business. I tried some of his coyote gland lure and "Predator Pulse" bait recently and they put a hurting on old wiley. Another good all-around predator lure is Paul Dobbin's "Canine Select." I believe that all of the lure makers I have covered make mink lures loaded with mink musk and beaver lures with beaver castor. All of these lures are good change-up lures for coyotes.

Good Books on Trapping & Snaring Coyotes
1 – "Hoofbeats of A Wolfer" – L. Craig O'Gorman
2 – "Desert Trapping of the Big Three" – J.C. Conner
3 – "The Dirt Hole and Its Variations" – Charles Dobbins
4 – "The Flat Set" – Charles Dobbins
5 – "Dynamite Snares and Snaring" – Tom Krause
6 – "Leggett's Coyote Trapping" – Ron & Pete Leggett
7 – "Trapping The Elusive Ones" – Mike Marsyada
8 – "Coyote Fever" – Ray Milligan
9 – "Active Trappers Method of Fox & Coyote Trapping"
   – Neil Olson
10 – "Predator Trapping Problems & Solutions" – Slim Pederson
11 – "Master Land Snaring" – Newt Sterling

12 – "Longline Coyote Trapping" – Garold Weiland
13 – "Coyote Man – Ray Alcorn" – Major Boddicker
14 – "Catchin Coyotes & Other Critters" – Major Boddicker
15 – "Coyote Trapping with Smitty" – R.C. Smith
16 – "Grawes Snaring Methods" – A.M. Grawe
17 – "Trapping The Eastern Brush Wolf" – Russ Carman
18 – "Dynamite Predator Trapping" – Tom Krause
19 – "Coyote Hunting & Trapping Primer – Gerry Lavigne &
    Bob Noonan

Coyote Trapping Videos

O'Gorman, Milligan, Derrick, Graham, Dakoto Line and others
have good videos out on trapping and snaring coyotes. Go to their
websites or catalogs for listings. Bob Noonan's video "Coyote Trapping 101" can be very helpful to beginners and can be ordered from
Trapper's Post magazine.

Trapping Magazines

1 - Fur-Fish-Game
    2878 East Main Street
    Columbus, OH 43209
    (614) 231-9585

2 - Trapper's Post
    P.O. Box 129
    Canaan, ME 04924
    (207) 660-2380

3 - Trapper's World
    P.O. Box 96
    Galloway, OH 43119
    (614) 878-6011

4 – Trap & Trail
   32596 Cty. Road 13
   Houston, MN 55943
   (507) 429-2227

Trapperman Website

Paul Dobbins hosts this website that is viewed by trappers from all over North America. There is a trapper's forum where trappers share their thoughts and ideas with others. You can find where used trapper's supplies are sold and there is a page for trapper's tips. This is a great website. Go online to www.trapperman.com.

Trapping Associations

There are currently two national-level trapping associations and most states have state level associations. These associations work at organizing trappers, hosting educational seminars, holding rendezvous, generating fur sales, and working with wildlife agencies and legislators to preserve the heritage of trapping and to protect trappers' rights. If you are interested in learning about coyotes and other furbearers or controlling coyotes, these associations have much to offer.

   Fur Takers of America
   P.O. Box 98
   Oregon, WI
   (608) 298-3119

   National Trappers Association
   2815 Washington Ave.
   Bedford, IN 47421
   (812) 277-9670

You can go online and search for individual state trappers' associations.

Coyote Calling Gear & Info

Having the right gear and learning how to use it is the first
step in becoming a successful coyote and predator hunter. There are
so many calls of all kinds on the market today that it can be both
mind-boggling and confusing to the beginner. A good coyote caller
can lure in coyotes with most any call that's sold, but those of us
who control coyotes on a regular basis have our favorites.

I may have mentioned before that I do a lot of calling using
mouth-blown calls, but I do use an electronic caller at times. Currently I use a call made by Icotec. I was so impressed with the
sound, the functioning and the fair pricing of their calls that I
became a field representative and dealer for them. There are other
good electronic callers and some junk on the market today, but I
highly recommend and endorse Icotec products.

The cow horn coyote howler that I am so fond of was made by
Herb Brussman of Oregon. Herb has been a knowledgeable, bona
fide coyotero all of his life and is now retired.

Many moons ago I came up with the idea of using a diaphragm
mouth call to imitate the rabbit distress calls that myself and so
many others used to call in coyotes. I had been using them for some
time to call in turkeys and also to make the bugling sound of an elk.
I kept at it until I got the sound I wanted, tried them out on foxes,
bobcats and coyotes all over the U.S., and they worked great. I've
even called in a bear and a lion or two with them. I believe I am
the first predator hunter to use these calls and probably the first to
win a predator-calling contest while using them. I could be wrong,
though.

For several years I sold these diaphragm calls along with my
own brand of wooden tube calls under the name of Superior Predator Calls. I still sell a few of the diaphragm calls if and when I do a
predator-calling seminar. After several years passed, I started seeing
predator call companies selling them. Torry Cook of MFK Game

Calls sent me some that he is now using and selling and they are terrific. Torry is a real coyote caller.

Major Boddicker of Colorado came out with a line of predator calls (Crit R Calls) in the mid 1970s that have caused many a coyote to bite the dust. I have had good success with all of his calls, but am particularly fond of his "Song Dog" howler call. I will switch from my old cow horn howler to the Song Dog at times to get a different sound out to the coyotes. Major is another top-gun coyotero and his calls and products are first class.

Ed Sceery hails from New Mexico and has been producing predator and game calls for many years. Like Boddicker and other serious coyoteros, he has not only killed many coyotes, he has studied them. Just because someone can shoot coyotes or other game, this does not make him a master hunter, woodsman or coyotero. Those who have been "students" of coyotes for many years and also have common sense are the best of the coyoteros. I have used Ed's products for a long time and recommend them highly.

Good Coyote Calling Books
1 – *Calling East & West* – Gerry Blair
2 – *Crit R Calling With The Major* – Major Boddicker
3 – *Talking To Coyotes With The Song Dog* – Major Boddicker
4 – *The Predator Callers Companion* – Gerry Blair
5 – *The Voice of The Coyote* – Frank Dobie
This is not a "how to" or methods book, but one worth reading to learn about coyotes.

Major Boddicker (Crit R Calls) also sells CDs and cassettes that are very informative. Ed Sceery offers a DVD, *Science of Predator Calling,* that can teach you much about calling coyotes and other predators. One can go on Icotec's website and view videos made by their expert caller, J.D. Piatt.

Back fifty or sixty years ago, Burnham Brothers and Johnny Stewart were the "kings" of predator calling, and both outfits produced calls that lured in hundreds of thousands of coyotes. When I first started calling in game I used them with good results. I used the old Circe and Tally Ho coyote calls and found them to be very effective. I once used Fox Pro electronic callers with good results. I know that there are other good coyote calls on the market today such as Primo's, Zepps, Knight & Hale, Haydel's and others that I've never used which is why I don't personally endorse them. But that does not mean that they are not good calls.

I often use trail cameras on coyote research projects.
This coyote was moving in daylight.

Where To Buy Coyote Calls & Gear

Icotec
6415 Angola Rd.
Holland, Oh 43528
(419) 450-3566

Southeastern Outdoor Supplies, Inc.
4250 Figsboro Rd.
Martinsville, VA 24112
(276) 638-4698

Crit R Calls
Rocky Mountain Wildlife Products
P.O. Box 999
La Porte, CO 80535
(877) 484-2768

Sceery's Outdoors
P.O. Box 6520
Santa Fe, N.M. 87502
1-800-327-4322

MFK Game Calls
Torry Cook
mfkgamecalls.com
(870) 463-8708

Cattleman Raymond Chernault hoists one of the Briery Creek coyotes.

CHAPTER 17

The Coyotes of Briery Creek Hollow

THE FARMHANDS AND OWNERS of two cattle farms that border Briery Creek told me that they were seeing a goodly number of coyotes hanging around the cow pastures. Coyotes were singing their songs on a regular basis at night and were quite bold about hanging around the barns and corrals. Cows were ready to start dropping calves and the stockmen were getting worried.

I worked on both of these farms on a yearly basis and had trimmed the coyote numbers down considerably. The number of calves lost to coyotes had been reduced to near nothing because of my efforts, and everyone involved wanted it to stay that way. I like to refer to this kind of coyote control as preventative maintenance. It makes my job easier and less pressured and the livestock producers lose less of their profits. It's a win-win situation for everyone involved, except old wiley.

Most of the larger farm was fenced with woven wire, which can help the coyotero do his job by guarding all crawl-under-the-fence holes with snares. Hanging a snare over one of these holes is much easier than digging in the ground to set foothold traps. Also, I don't have to deal with worrisome livestock setting off my traps. I cruised the fence line and set about half dozen snares.

It has never been my policy to set high numbers of traps on anyplace, but I do like to set enough in key locations to knock out

A Briery Creek coyote tried to slip under a fence and got snared.

as many coyotes as quickly as possible. It doesn't take the average coyote long to wise up to what's going on. They are quick learners. On this farm, I made seven foothold sets at proven locations. Where a woods road connected two large pastures, I made two sets. In a draw that crossed a small stream leading from one pasture to another, I put in two more sets. On a high ridge where a draw began, I made two sets, and I made another set near a narrowed-down choke point between pastures.

I mix my sets up—some dirthole, some peep hole and a flat set or two. I'll use a T-bone or grab-and-die stick at a flat set on occasions. I don't like to overdo any one set, and I'm a believer in using different baits and smells at sets. I don't use urine at every set, but when I do I use coyote, bobcat and fox urine. I have never seen where it made much difference except when making a urine post set. If it's a urine post set for coyotes, I use coyote urine. Quite often I'll make a large dirthole set, bait it with a good bait (fresh or prepared), lure it with cat gland scent and give it a good shot of cat urine. This set will take both cats and canines.

After I finished setting this farm, I drove around the other farm and picked out locations for four sets. I didn't set any of them as it was near dark and I had a thirty-mile drive home. This farm was just across a highway from the one I'd set, and I knew the same group of coyotes were hunting on both of them. This farm was more difficult to set because all of the fences were high tensile wire affairs and coyotes could go through the wire anywhere they chose to. I found no snare locations except for cow paths, but I never set snares in these locations when there are cows using the pasture. Cow paths have always proven to be deadly coyote locations when using either snares or foothold traps, but it's not worth the headache if cows are using them. These paths are also good for catching fox, and when the paths ramble around through thick areas of undergrowth, they can be good bobcat locations as well.

Leaving home well before daylight the following morning, I stopped on the way to make a few howls on another place I would work on in a few days. No coyotes answered my howls, nor did I see any. I kill a few coyotes every year doing this. Even at times when I don't get an answering howl, sometimes a coyote will pop out in the open to eyeball the area, looking for an intruder.

I checked empty traps and snares on the farm I'd set the day before until I came to the next to last fence snare. A big dog coyote met his Waterloo there and I was pleased. Later I weighed the beast and he tipped the scales at 47½ pounds. We get quite a few eastern coyotes that weigh 15–20 pounds more than that. I cut tissue samples off of the tips of their tongues and these are sent to a well-known university for DNA studies. Most of these big coyotes have wolf genes in them, some may have domestic dog in them and some have all three. These devils can pull down a lot of livestock and deer.

It irritates me when I hear wildlife officials telling the public that these eastern coyotes rarely kill larger calves and mature deer. They need to leave their desks and computers behind and spend time out there with coyotes to see what really goes on. Very few of these people will even listen to what the professional coyote men tell them. The trend now is for some of these officials to tell people that there are "good" coyotes and "bad" coyotes! It is true that some coyotes have never killed livestock and some never will. Why? It's because they never had to or never had the opportunity.

I made four sets, all with foothold traps on the farm across the road. These sets were made where a farm lane intersected the main road going in about halfway through the farm. A cross fence at this location called for two gate openings, which made it even better. In the dry mud, I spotted several sets of coyote tracks heading in all directions. From the start, I chose this location even before I saw the tracks. A coyote man who wants to stay in business learns to spot such locations easily once he has some experience under his belt. I knew that these four sets would produce more coyotes than a dozen sets scattered all over the farm.

Many aspiring coyote trappers read of roadways, farm lanes, trails, field edges, fence lines, hedgerows, pond dams and draws as the place to make sets. The problem most have is in choosing the best of these places. There are generally dozens of such locations like those mentioned on every place you'll go to trap. If conditions are favorable for seeing sign, this will make it easier. But I set many locations where I don't see sign because I know from experience that these are the places where the coyotes will travel. The more you learn about coyotes and the better you become at reading terrain, the easier it will become for you when choosing locations.

Those of us who spend our lives in the outdoors encounter and see things that are sometimes comical and sometimes strange. One day I had begun checking traps on the larger farm and saw I had

Coyotes like to chew the ears off of cows and calves.

caught a female coyote in the draw right behind the landowner's house and was pleased. I then headed down into the bottom lands that bordered Briery Creek. Another coyote off this farm would sure make my day.

Looking across the bottom land pasture, I could see an animal in one of the traps where the road that linked the two fields began. I was several hundred yards away but I could see that the animal was of good size and dark gray in color. I headed that way. About halfway there I noticed that the trapped critter was not jumping up and down but rolling around, and I then knew it had to be a coon. Was he a whopper! I believe he was the largest coon I've ever caught in the east and figured he would weigh well over twenty-five pounds.

Just as I pulled up to the location, I spotted a skunk leaving the area where my other trap was set, heading to pass right by the coon. The coon made a lunge at the skunk and the devil whirled around and let go of a full load of essence in the old coon's face! The skunk then ambled off into the woods, in no hurry at all, and the smell enveloped my truck. I wanted to weigh that huge coon and would have had the hide tanned if he was prime, but he wasn't. I wasn't about to waste that big, beautiful coon for nothing, so I finally wrestled him down with my choke pole, released him and got the heck out of there! The following morning I had a young female coyote in the trap across from the coon catch site and remade that set and the one where the coon was caught.

The four sets on the farm across the road produced a double on coyotes about three days after they had been set. I caught a total of six coyotes, two red fox and a couple of coons on the big farm. Of the eight coyotes taken, the largest was a male that weighed fifty-three and three-quarters pounds and the smallest was a five- to six-month-old female that weighed twenty-two and one-half pounds. I carry an accurate set of scales that I can hang from a limb to weigh the critters for my research records. I am anxious to find out how much wolf (and maybe dog) that big coyote had in his gene pool.

These animals were caught in the time frame of a week. In some of the areas I trap it might have taken 10 or 12 days to catch eight coyotes if they were traveling a larger range. But the Briery Creek coyotes were hanging close to those calving cows, looking for an easy meal. As far as I know, no calves were lost on either place this season to coyotes and the stockmen were very pleased with my work. And I was a happy old coyotero!

A Briery Creek cow gives a coyote the bad eye.

Cattleman Russell Harper holds one of the Campus Coyotes.

CHAPTER 18

Campus Coyotes

WHILE I WAS ATTENDING COLLEGE on a hit-or-miss basis many moons ago, I don't recall ever seeing a coyote in a classroom studying for a degree. But not so long ago, a small-town policeman contacted me about a group of coyotes that were quite frequently hanging around a university campus. Some of the college crowd thought it was the neatest thing since sliced bread; others feared for the safety of the students and faculty.

I had already been contracted to deal with some calf-chasing coyotes on two farms not far from the school and had a hunch it would be the same group of wild canines. In years past I had performed coyote control on one of the farms, and the new farm of about 200 acres was within one-half mile of the campus and about one-and-one-half miles from the other farm. After doing some scouting and talking to people who lived in the area, I was sure that my hunch was correct.

These puppies had a good setup. They had two cattle farms and several hundreds of acres of dense thickets scattered about that were teeming with deer and other wildlife to feed on. A busy four-lane highway nearby also produced a steady supply of road kills, mostly deer. There was little hunting activity in the area and no trapping whatsoever. And then I got the big news—some students on campus had been feeding the coyotes! To top that off, people in all of the neighborhoods between the farms and the college were losing cats and small dogs at an alarming rate.

Well, I wasn't about to make coyote sets on campus. I think all of us are aware of the number of liberal, anti-students (and faculty) who hang around colleges these days. If they caught me in the act of harming a coyote eating cheeseburgers, pizza and such, I would surely die a slow, agonizing death! My coyote control would have to be performed quietly and out of sight. This was the first time I was called on to do "covert" coyote control. The farms were behind locked gates and this helped my situation. Here I would terminate the junk food coyotes.

The farm the greatest distance (about two miles) from the college was where I began operations. I put in two sets in a wide-open creek bottom (pasture) that cut through the middle of the farm, near a fence that bordered a wooded area. I generally caught two-three coyotes at this location every year. The sets were deadly if only the aggravating cows would leave them alone. I hate it, but cow-tripped traps are part of catching coyotes in pastures. Once in a while I'll find a pasture that will have some areas outside the wire that provide good set locations, but this place didn't. A cutover thicket of several hundreds of acres separated this farm from the one closest to the college, but it was off limits to everyone.

A cow died giving birth to a calf and I had the farmhands move it with one of their big tractors to the far back corner of the pasture where it bordered the big thicket. I knew the coyotes would lay up in the nearby brush and come out to feed on the dead livestock and gorge themselves. They probably preferred this set up over the sorry cheeseburger and pizza deal on campus.

I had a barbed-wire fence to deal with instead of woven wire, so there were no hot crawl-under holes to hang snares over. Within two days coyote fur was found hanging all up and down the barbed wire. By using a natural, existing growth and adding just a little of my own, I soon had two snare locations. Two foothold traps were set out fifty feet or more from the carcass. I knew I'd be looking at caught coyotes in short order if all went well.

Moving on to the next farm, I made three sets (footholds) where a large (12' x 8') concrete culvert passed under the four-lane highway. Every animal around, including deer, used this tunnel. I made my standard array of sets—a large dirthole, a two-peephole set, and a grab-and-die stick set out about forty feet from the edge of the culvert where a farm lane crossed the tiny stream. It doesn't get much better than this for locations.

Crossing a large hay field, I made two sets at one end of a large pond dam and then dropped down to a weedy area that bordered a large creek. The owners had bush hogged a six-foot trail through the high weeds and were using it as a four-wheeler path. Two more sets were put in, one on each side of the travel way. I had never set this farm before but I knew I had it covered well with seven sets. The next day I did find a stretch of woven wire that bordered the four-lane and put in a snare to guard a hole in the wire. Adjoining the hay field was a large pasture where the cows and calves stayed, and I didn't see any need to set there.

Daybreak the next morning found me on the farm where the dead cow was located. One coyote was dead in one of the fence snares and a very lively one was jumping up and down in an MB550. I drew a blank in the wide open creek bottom and headed for the next farm. I looked at empty sets until I reached the two in the path near the creek. A big male was caught there. I was pleased with the first night's catch. Three coyotes out of thirteen sets was fine with me. I set the snare in the fence where I'd found the hole and headed home.

Although I trap year around for coyotes, I'm sure not a high roller anymore. We only trap coyotes for pay and will still kill two or three hundred coyotes a year. My old body won't go like it used to, and I've found that when I push myself too hard, I begin to not like what I do. We also turn down jobs that require a lot of driving as I get so stiff in my knees and hip I can hardly walk after long stretches of windshield time.

When the weather is warm, rarely do I have more than a dozen or two sets out. When it gets colder, I may run up to fifty sets, maybe more, counting snares. When I was running this particular little line, we had a skim of frost some mornings but it would heat up to 70° or more before noon. Working in hot weather is hard on this old coyotero. I've been in the trapping game for 60 years now and have to slow down whether I want to or not. Thanks to the experience I have and what I've learned over the years from some mighty good coyote men, I don't have to work as hard or set as many traps as some do to catch the same number of coyotes.

In a week's time I caught four more coyotes. Two were caught in the farm lane in front of the culvert, one was snared in the hole in the wire by the four-lane and one was finally caught in the wide open creek bottom. After that everything went cold, and after a few days of catching nothing more, I pulled up. I'm sure I didn't catch all of the campus coyotes, but there were seven fewer of them to chase calves and eat junk food (and pets).

In the past twenty years, I have learned that coyotes anywhere can survive in high numbers on relatively small territories when the food supply is ample. Also, there are fewer coyote men out there keeping their numbers thinned down and there will be even fewer good coyoteros in the future. Most of the younger crowd will not stick with what it takes to become professionals. It can be a trying and demanding occupation that seldom provides high pay and secure benefits.

Even with the hard knocks and poverty I've experienced as a trapper, I don't regret a minute of it. I heartily agree with an old trapper (I can't remember his name) who once wrote — "I was born a trapper, I shall live as a trapper and die a trapper!"

The Campus Coyotes really enjoyed chasing calves.

Brother Ben with his first coyote on the ground tries for another.

CHAPTER 19

First Coyote

Y OU KNOW, WHEN A MAN PAYS for an airline ticket to fly across the U.S. just to kill a coyote, there just might be a little something wrong with that fellow. But when two men do this and take their wives along and put them up in a high-class hotel, I think you might could get a shrink or a judge to declare them insane. The old saying "his elevator doesn't go all the way to the top" certainly applies to the two men who did such a thing.

I almost hate to admit to this, but I was one of those men. Before this incident took place, I had spent a good portion of my life in the wild west chasing coyotes and other critters. I was back east trapping for fur ,and my brother Benji started this whole thing about going out west to call coyotes, which gives me the right to blame most of this deal on him. At that time, I don't think he'd ever been out west, but since he was a kid he'd been in love with that part of the world. Of course, listening to his older brother's tales of excitement and adventure out west only fanned the fires. Looking at photos of pickup loads of coyotes taken by his brother and those he hunted with drove the poor boy to the edge, I think.

Brother Ben was an avid deer hunter, but the eastern deer seasons were over, the weather was miserable, he didn't trap like I did and his mind began scheming. He would usually drop in late in the evenings when I'd be in Pa's shop skinning beavers, otters, coons, muskrats, bobcats and foxes I'd caught that day. Oh, he'd prance back and forth in the shop getting in my way and talk about how he'd just watched the national weather station and saw that the temperature was 65° in southern Arizona and how nice it would be to be there calling in coyotes.

He knew that I had a real weakness for calling Arizona coyotes. He'd heard me tell dozens of stories of Gerry Blair and I calling and shooting coyotes west of Wickenburg and other parts of the state. He knew that I had often talked about moving permanently to Arizona or New Mexico where both coyotes and mountain lions were plentiful. I have to admit, the boy had a good scheme and it worked. Here I was slogging around in ice-choked beaver swamps when I could have been in sunny Arizona, calling coyotes or looking for lions.

It didn't take very much convincing and hardly any lying to convince our wives that we foursome should go and soak up some Arizona rays. Shucks, these two poor gals were not accustomed to their redneck husbands taking them on far-away trips! Airline tickets were bought, reservations were made at an upscale resort just out of Phoenix and soon we were on our way.

After arriving in Phoenix, we rented a vehicle, drove to the resort and checked in. If I remember correctly, we took them out to dine that night at a high-class restaurant and really put the dog on, so to speak. They were excited about staying at a place where the swimming pool was open in February and looked forward to shopping in nearby shops and being pampered a bit. Brother Ben and I were thinking only about going after coyotes. We would have been just as happy sleeping out under the bright desert stars and eating fried bologna, but we figured we had to play the game and be the best of husbands.

An hour before daylight the next morning, we were finishing up breakfast at a small café in Wickenburg, a small town about an hour's drive west of Phoenix. Just before daylight we parked the vehicle on the side of a lonely gravel road that snaked its way through a huge greasewood flat. I laid my head back, let go of a mournful voice howl and listened. No coyote answered and I was disappointed. I wanted Ben to see how howling can work.

We made calling stands throughout the morning and only glimpsed a coyote or two at first. Then I did call in a coyote that went by us so fast we never got a shot off! My brother was awed by the number of rabbits, both cottontail and jacks, that would respond to the call and sit around us. Later in the day we left the flat country and headed north into the hills around Congress, an old mining town. From here we traveled into rugged mountains that rose higher and higher as we neared Flagstaff. Ben was awed by the breathtaking scenery and how the country could change so quickly. It's good to see the western country on TV or the movies, but you have to go there to really experience the quietness, the harshness and the grandeur of it all.

All the while we were traveling, I had been pondering on why we had seen so few coyotes. Then it dawned on my slow-working brain! Here we were in February when most coyotes were mated up and preparing to raise young ones. I'm sure the hunters (callers) and trappers had made a big dent in the coyote population that fall and winter. I remembered someone once telling me that coyote calling contests were often held around the Wickenburg area. Shucks, by now the remaining coyotes were wizened up and could probably identify the brands of calls I was using.

This called for a new strategy and I soon had a plan. It was getting late in the afternoon, and I headed back towards Phoenix, hoping to find a spot closer to town where the average caller or trapper doesn't like to operate in. I found such a spot and we passed through a BLM gate, parking the car out of sight. We quietly eased our way about a half a mile down the rough road until I found what

I thought would be a suitable place. I put Ben into position with the old 12-gauge pump, I backed off a bit and let go of some terrible dying rabbit screams. Within two or three minutes the shotgun roared and my brother had taken his first coyote. He was happy, but I believe I was happier.

After taking a few pictures we hung the beast from the limb of a Palo Verde tree and skinned him out. We had brought along some plastic bags and a cooler to take care of such things. We arrived back in Phoenix just after dark, cleaned up and took the ladies out for another fine dinner. That first trip out west (and the first coyote) had a lasting effect on my brother. Since that time, he has traveled all over the west many times, and he even bought a piece of land in Arizona. He began to realize why his nomadic brother longed to be in such places and often turned his back on civilization.

We cruised around the state with the girls, even going into California just to say they had been there. At one remote place we stopped and I did a bit of poking around in a nearby sand wash and showed my brother the first lion track he'd ever seen. We encountered snow flurries one day in Wickenburg, and all of the locals were really excited. They hadn't seen the white stuff in years. It reminded me of the foot or more of snow that I'd be trudging through in the Blue Ridge hill country once we arrived back home. I had to get back to the trapline.

Farm manager Mike Randolph checks out a dead calf–chasing coyote.

This fall coyote's fur is not fully prime but his color is nice.

CHAPTER 20

A Fall Coyote Line

THE MAMA COW, A BIG, BLOCKY ANGUS, did her best to protect her newborn calf. But her efforts were futile in the end. Two or more coyotes fought her, biting and grabbing at her heels, nose or whatever they could, while one or two coyotes killed the calf quickly with bites to the neck. The calf's stomach was ripped open even before it stopped breathing. From the looks of things, other cows came to the rescue (too late) and ran the hellish beasts away.

This was the second calf killed by coyotes in this pasture of about 300 acres in the past week. I got back into my truck to finish off a cup of coffee and take a smoke before going to work. Nearly every time I deal with grizzly scenes such as this one, I can't help but think of all the so-called wildlife "experts" who tell people that coyotes eat or kill only the old, sickly, crippled or weak animals. They tell people that they may kill a young sheep or fawn deer on rare occasion, but rarely attack or kill healthy animals. I wish to hell that some of these know-it-alls had to follow me around for a few days.

Believe it or not, I don't hate coyotes or any other predator. They do have their role to play in the scheme of life itself. In some areas where I've trapped, they have actually helped landowners by cutting down on the deer population. Coyotes and other predators have also provided for a good portion of my income, along with pesky beavers. I have access to many thousands of acres of private land, much of it behind locked gates, where I'm allowed to hunt, fish and trap as a result of being a predator and beaver trapper.

Having trapped this farm before, I knew where most of my traps would be set. First on the agenda was to put in two sets out about 50 feet from the calf carcass (what was left of it). Even when there's nothing left to eat, the coyotes will still come by to sniff around and urinate. I generally put in a standard dirthole set and then a flat or peephole set. I've been at this game long enough to know that these standard sets, using standard smells, will not always catch the older dogs that have seen these sorts of sets before. But they will almost always account for the younger and uneducated ones, or at least some of them.

After setting on both calf carcasses, I then headed for the back corner of the pasture. Here I hung a snare in a hole in the fence. Over the years, I've taken eight or ten coyotes here. About 20 yards from the snare set, I put in a walk-through set in a cow path. A dab of skunk essence was smeared on an overhanging limb, about four feet above ground, over the well-blended set.

Next I placed an old bleached and battered cow skull at the base of a thick, sticky clump of hog weed, about 15-20 yards away from the snare and walk-through set. My trap was blended in about 10" out from the skull and I used clumps of grass about 2" high to frame the trap in. Placed properly, these clumps most always put the paw on the pan. A gob of pure mink musk was put down in one eye socket of the skull. Neither the walk-through nor the skull set had any urine applied anywhere.

I took a ride around the big pasture, but I didn't set any more traps. There really was no need to. In my younger years, I would have probably put in another six or eight sets at "good looking" locations. Years of experience have taught me that a few, quality (and diversified) sets set on the *right* location were all that was needed.

After all of these years chasing and studying coyotes,
I still get a thrill out of hearing them howl.

All others would be a waste of energy and time. The smart trapper learns to spot or "sense" these top-producing locations, whether he sees sign or not.

The first week of October on this line turned warm, so I hastened to another cow farm owned by the same folks. Setting traps in hot weather is definitely not as enjoyable as setting in cold weather for fur. But when most of the gold you earn comes from chasing stock-killing coyotes, you learn to go with the flow. Warm-weather coyote trapping usually means fewer catches for more work, but the man is paying you to stop the killing, so you do your best and don't complain. It still beats a "real" job.

The next farm, about five miles down the road, was a sportsman's paradise. I sat atop a high ridge overlooking open low grounds bordering a small river and spotted a flock of turkeys feeding. The leaves on the maple, gum, hickory and poplar trees that covered a steep bluff in the distance were mixed hues of yellow, red, green and gold. Fall was upon us for sure. It made this old woodsbum's heart happy just to be able to gaze upon these splendors of nature.

A dozen or so fat cows, along with their frolicking calves, came out of the woods to graze and I came out of my trance. I was here to keep those little calves alive and needed to get to work. Coyotes had been spotted feeding on a dead cow by one of the farm workers several days ago, and I drove over near the bloated carcass.

A quick search revealed several piles of fresh coyote scat. The entrails and most of the meat had been eaten from the carcass by vultures, crows and the coyotes, but I knew that every coyote in the country would visit this site for several months to come. Long after the "goodies" were gone, the wild dogs would stop by to sniff around and urinate. I put three sets in at this location. I never set traps up close to a carcass, as I don't want to catch buzzards, hawks, etc.

I drove across the pasture to a woods road that ran through a large strand of hardwoods and led to another pasture. Several more turkeys and a small buck deer were spotted feeding on acorns in the hardwoods. In this part of the country, white oak acorns are much sought after by both deer and turkeys. The old woods road would be a prime place to hunt for winter meat in a month or so.

Small bands of cattle and calves were scattered all over the next pasture, and a trip around the perimeter, along the fence, produced no hot or surefire locations to hang snares. Most of the pasture was fenced with three or four strands of barbwire and the coyotes could come and go into the pasture wherever they pleased. I settled on making three sets where the woods road joined the pasture. Coyotes would use the road going from one pasture to the next.

The October sun was beginning to dip lower in the west when I finished these three sets, and I decided to head home to get chores done before dark. I was about 40 miles from home. My greatest dislike for doing ADC all over the country is the driving involved. When really busy, I may have to travel 150 miles or more with several jobs going. Being as I'm now in my "golden years," I don't care for a lot of driving at night on roads I'm unfamiliar with.

I ran into the farm manager on my way out, and he was pleased to see me on the job. "Guess you'll knock 'em dead tonight, huh?" he commented. Laughing, I explained to him that coyote trapping was often a waiting game. Coyotes in this part of the country often travel five to ten square miles. If you happen to set just ahead of them, you may pick up several on the first night. If you set just behind them, you will more than likely wait a few nights for a catch. In the spring when the female is raising young, neither she nor her mate will travel far, but by fall, they're on the go.

The next day I had a couple of coons in the sets around the calf carcasses and nothing else. There was a time when I'd catch several foxes off each of the farms, but the increasing number of coyotes put a stop to this. What few foxes remained stayed close to the houses and farm buildings or deep in the thickets. I traveled on to another farm and made half a dozen sets, two by a calf carcass that was the result of a birthing death, not coyotes. But the devils wasted no time in eating up the tender veal.

About half the carcasses I set on anywhere are not coyote kills. The coyotes will do their share of killing, but often get blamed for far more than they actually kill. On the other hand, I've had cow farmers tell me that they have coyotes go through a herd and never bother or get after anything. They are soon convinced that coyotes don't kill calves or sheep. When they tell me this I only chuckle and say that they are lucky—for now. Sooner or later, when old wiley gets the right chance, he or she's gonna grab hold to something. A coyote can't help but be a coyote.

On the fourth night I finally connected with coyotes on the first farm I'd set up. Had a brush wolf in the fence snare, one in a nearby flat set and one in a dirthole set by a calf carcass where I'd caught one of the coons earlier. The second farm produced one coyote and the third nothing.

The next day produced a pair of yotes on the second farm and a pair on the third. For four or five days after that, I looked at empty traps. On many of these places now I rarely catch a skunk or possum. Like the foxes that have survived, they stay out of the open pastures. This has helped me in two ways. One, they don't screw up my coyote sets. Two, I often get paid well for trapping skunks that have taken up residence under people's houses.

After having to reset four or five times (the result of nosey cows), the trap at the walk-through set by the fence produced a big male coyote on farm number one. Another coyote was caught in the fence snare.

Farm number two produced a total of four coyotes and number three produced five. I caught a total of 13 coyotes on three farms in roughly two weeks. The calf killing stopped, and the coyotes stayed shy of these farms. The farm manager and owner said I must have caught them all, but I knew better. Maybe I had taken a little better than half of them. Any honest coyote man will tell you that rarely does any trapper, regardless of his skill, ever catch them all.

The ADC coyote man plays a much different game than does the high-rolling, longline fur trapper. While trapping these three farms, I never had out more than 24 traps or snares. I made several attempts at calling and howling them in but was skunked on this end. Sometimes I get one or two from calling, and I consider these to be a bonus. A man has to use every tool or skill available when dealing with coyotes. They learn fast. The older ones that survive tend not to forget much.

The fall weather held good on that job, the cow farmers were happy and I was paid very well for my efforts. But the phone had been ringing and I had other coyotes to chase at other places. Seems like everybody has a coyote or varmint problem of some sort these days. But I'm not complaining—it keeps me out there where I want to be.

This coyote sports a beautiful coat.

The coyote bayed the bear like a bear hound would have.

CHAPTER 21

The Coyote & The Bear

IT WAS HOT. The clock in the truck dash showed that it was around noon, the temperature was already 90° and not a breath of air stirred anywhere. I was slowly cruising around a large pasture on a cattle farm, checking the woven wire fence for places where calf-eating coyotes were entering the field, and I was making a turn at a fence corner when I heard what I thought at first to be a dog barking its fool head off, down in the woods on the other side of the fence.

I stopped the truck and listened. The constant, rapid barking never let up. After listening a bit, I got out of the truck, walked over to the fence and listened more. Soon I came to the conclusion that it was not a domestic dog doing all of the hell raising, but a coyote! In all of my years in the woods, anywhere in America, I had never heard a single coyote bark this much. I was puzzled to say the least. It was June, and knowing that female coyotes were with pups, I figured these crazy goings-on had to be related to a female with pups.

All of this action was taking place about 100 yards or more down in some thick pine and brush growth, and I couldn't see what was going on. After another five minutes or so of this constant yammering, I couldn't take it anymore. Grabbing my rifle, I eased over the fence and began stalking towards the upset coyote. Easing along, slowly and quietly, I got within 50 yards of the coyote and could see a little through the thick growth. The coyote was baying at something in a thick clump of brush, running back and forth in front of it.

Movement beyond the coyote caught my eye, and I soon could pick out the heads of two coyote pups, peering over a fallen log, watching Mama doing her thing. I could only catch glimpses of the female coyote as she dodged back and forth in front of the brush clump. I remember wishing that I had brought along my old 870 Remington pump loaded with #4 buckshot and not the scoped rifle.

I was just starting to move a little to my right to see better when I felt a slight breeze hit the back of sweaty neck, going straight to the coyote. Damn! I knew my goose was cooked for sure.

A black bear, weighing maybe 300 pounds, rose up from the clump of brush, turned and looked straight at me! The coyote stopped the barking and froze in her tracks. I was so startled at what was taking place that I froze in my tracks also. Before I could get myself together and even raise my rifle to try and get the coyote in my scope, the bear let out a loud "woof." Dropping back down quickly, the bear picked up something in its mouth and crashed away through the brush at top speed.

I caught a fleeting glimpse of the coyote as she took out behind the bear. Soon she began barking again like a bear hound running a hot track. I never saw the pups again and figured they were some-where behind her. I just stood there, like a big dummy, trying to figure out what the hell I had just witnessed.

Coming out of my stupor, I walked down to the brush where the bear had been. I could still hear the fool coyote, a quarter of a mile or more away, still barking occasionally at the bear. I saw hair and bits and pieces of a fawn deer where the bear had apparently been feeding on it.

Then I started asking myself questions. Why was this coyote, with pups, acting such a fool as to try and run a bear off of the fawn? Did the bear kill the fawn or did the coyote? To the best I could figure it, the coyote killed the fawn and was going to share it with the pups. The bear, who must have been nearby, came in and took it away from her. Why else would a lone coyote (or even a pack of them) take on a bear?

Like many other happenings that I have witnessed in a lifetime in the woods, I realize I'll never know for sure how this particular event came down. I did tell one of my bear-hunting buddies about the incident and told him that if I ever caught this coyote, I could take her alive and sell her to him to put in his bear pack.

The foot hold traps that we use merely hold or restrain the coyote. They do not cut off or mangle legs as the anti-trapping folks would have people to believe.

A duck eating coyote.

CHAPTER 22

A Tough Customer

O N HIS EARLY MORNING WALK around a part of his sprawling estate, the gentleman farmer witnessed a coyote grabbing a duck near the edge of a small pond and fleeing with it. The old fellow loved his ducks, sheep and chickens and was pretty upset. His farm manager suggested that he contact "the Shumaker" fellow and hire him to take care of the coyote problem. Within a few days, I was on the scene.

After taking a look-see around the estate, I started my job by putting in six sets around the small pond where dozens of ducks hung out. Two sets were put in on the dam of the pond, one on each side, and two along old cowpaths that followed the creek below the pond. On another part of the farm, I put in three sets where two farm lanes crossed. Hedgerows lined both roads.

On the third check I had a large, male coyote, hung up in one of the pond sets. The ducks were crowded all together out in the middle of the pond and raising hell. The next check produced a pair of coyotes at the crossroads location, and then the traps produced nothing for a week, so I pulled up. As a rule, I charge my customers for 10 days of trapping when dealing with coyotes. Depending on the range of the critters and food availability, it may take this long to catch any of them. My fee is based on a per-day, per-trip basis. Distance traveled factors in also.

Some ADC trappers charge a set fee for every animal caught and mileage. Out west, many coyote men are on salaries or contract year around. I found that an ADC trapper can go broke on a job when charging per animal only, especially when dealing with far-roaming coyotes or trap-shy beaver. Regardless of the skill of the trapper, he has no control over how animals travel, how many there are or what the weather has in store for him. When I'm on the job, I give it my best and have given many an extra day or two at no charge to get the job done. Rarely have I had an unhappy customer. And the referrals never end.

Learning all one can about the coyote—how to trap, kill and control them—is a lifetime of study in itself. My first encounter with coyotes came in the 60s, nearly half a century ago in Montana. We didn't have coyotes in Virginia back when I was a fledgling trapper. I've chased coyotes in several states in my life and have always had a desire to learn more about them. Trappers and hunters of all ages all over the country have helped with my coyote education. I'm very grateful to these people.

Most any average trapper can learn the basics of fox and coyote trapping, acquire the proper gear, go where there are coyotes and catch a few. I know many trappers who have caught a dozen or so coyotes (some accidently in fox sets) and think of themselves as authorities on the subject. I know of others who have caught a hundred in their lifetime and have been elevated by themselves and their peers as true gurus of coyote killing. Most of the real coyote men I've known couldn't tell you exactly how many they have accounted for. They may have a rough figure in their heads, but numbers and bragging are not important to them. Learning more about coyotes is what's important to them.

Yes, a coyote is a coyote to some extent. But are all coyotes equal or the same? No. Are some coyotes more unpredictable than others? Yes. Is the average coyote harder to trap than the average fox? No.

Sometimes two or more coyotes will get after a mama cow while another will grab her calf.

Is the trapper who catches 100 or more coyotes a season necessarily better than one who catches 20 a year? Not always so. The guy with the larger catch may have more and better territory, probably sets more traps and works longer and harder at the game. He may or may not have better skills than the other trapper.

I have spent a lifetime studying and catching predators and other furbearers. Will I ever know it all? No—no one ever will. The better trappers that I have known were thinkers, they were or are people who spend much of their time in the woods, year around. They constantly ponder and think of "what ifs." These trappers, by study, work, thought and effort, will catch as many coyotes in twelve traps as some who set fifty traps.

Kent Eanes, a Virginia trapper, has trapped for many years and is very accomplished, both on land and water. I'd put him up against most anybody. What amazes me about the guy is that he's always questioning somebody about trapping methods and wildlife. He knows more about both topics than any average trapper, but you'd never know it to hear him talk. He never stops wanting to learn and is completely "eat up" with trapping and has been all of his life. I have truly enjoyed his friendship and admire his ways.

If a coyote doesn't go by and see or smell your set, you won't catch him. Now that's almost a dumb statement, isn't it? But my point is this. Even if you have sets in good locations, the coyote or coyotes won't go by your sets on every trip through that area. Other smells, sightings, kills or items of interest may have caused them to miss your sets. But if you are patient and wait, sooner or later you're gonna get some of them. Haste often makes waste in coyote trapping.

Too many coyote trappers that I have known depend too much on bait or scent sets using foothold traps. An ADC man soon learns that some coyotes, often the ones doing the livestock killing, have learned to avoid most of these sets. The use of snares, blind sets with footholds, "trick sets" or calling is usually the answer for the wise ones. Many of the places I go on have been trapped by others, and it ain't always easy to kill the real troublemakers.

Killing or trapping shy coyotes separates the men from the boys, the wheat from the chaff. Many times over the years I have lost sleep and became downright miserable when dealing with these sort of boogers. Using any and everything I'd ever learned about controlling coyotes, I finally caught or killed many of them. But quite a few were never taken. It's gonna happen this way if you stay at it long, no matter how good you are. It's a fact of life for an ADC man.

I have spent weeks on catching or killing some coyotes. Maybe I should be ashamed to tell this, but I'm not. I don't think anyone else would have done much better, and I've been with some mighty good coyoteros. A lot of thought and patience on my part is usually what leads to the coyote's downfall.

A lot of what I'm writing or saying may sound like pure bull or nonsense to trappers who run short or long coyote lines for fur. They catch a few (the easier ones) and move one. What's the big deal? The big deal is that if they had to stay and catch all or most all of them, they would clearly understand what I'm rambling on about. It's a different ballgame.

Some time back I dealt with a coyote that was tougher than usual to catch. I had trapped several coyotes off of a place where pet dogs had vanished, chickens had been eaten and the wolfies had become bold enough to roam around in the people's yard and barn lot. All was well for several days after my initial catch, but then a lone coyote was spotted on a daily basis in the hay field behind the barn. I was never around with my trusty rifle when the yote made an appearance.

A farm road led through the middle of the hayfield, and I had several sets of various kinds along the road. I knew the coyote or any other coyote would travel this road — it's what coyotes do. If a trapper has learned what coyotes will do before they do it, half the battle is won. Tracks in the muddy lane revealed that this coyote walked by my sets on almost a daily basis but never broke stride. I slipped in a couple of blended-in flat sets with totally different smells, but the coyote ignored them.

The owners of the place had bought a puppy to replace one of the missing pets, but were afraid to let the pup roam free with the kids. Every day after I checked the traps, they met me in the driveway with expectant looks on their faces. They were sick of this lone coyote and so was I. Also, I was driving about 80 miles a day, round trip, to work this job. Gas ain't cheap.

After a fruitless check one morning, I sat in the truck in the farm lane and attempted to think of a way to end this. Blind set or snares? The terrain just wasn't suited for it. Calling and howling? I'd tried that with no success. I learned that every Bubba in the county owned an electronic game caller, and it was tough to even call in a young gray fox. Wolfies in this part of the country knew more about predator calling than I did.

My eyes finally settled on a small patch of brush, briars and weeds that was on one side of the farm lane where it entered a woodlot. A rock formation was here that prevented the half-acre-sized area from being used to grow hay. Bingo! A dim light came on in my feeble brain. That brush lot had to have a rabbit trail or two through it. I drove up to it and got busy, a ray of hope arising in my heart.

I found two or three well-used rabbit paths that started at the lane's edge and went into the thicket. About five feet off the lane a small bush was perfectly in place to hang a snare over the path. Ten or twelve feet beyond that I hung another snare. I had a groundhog carcass on the truck that had been taken in a small killer trap set over a hole under the owner's barn. I often do favors such as this for those I work for at no extra charge. It makes them happy and I get bait for traps. The hog was placed in the trail about 20 or 30 feet beyond the last snare. I covered it with a few handfuls of weeds to keep it from view of airborne vultures and hawks. I used no scent or urine anywhere. The hog would soon put out plenty of odor as the sun warmed up the countryside.

On the second night I hung a mature female coyote in the first snare. After that the coyote tracks in the lane vanished and the sightings in the hay field did also. The owners were happy, the kids were happy, the new puppy seemed happy and this old trapper sure as hell was happy!

The author remakes a set where a coyote was taken.

J.D. Piatt bagged this coyote with the aid of his Icotec electronic caller.

CHAPTER 23

High Tech Coyote Calling

I REMEMBER THINKING how splendid the coyote's fur looked as the last rays of a setting sun settled upon him. The coyote had just appeared out of a brushy draw in front of me and had the mean eye on a clump of prairie grass where my electronic call was concealed, the speaker belting out a chorus of the dying rabbit blues. The critter broke into a trot and headed for the sound of the distressed rabbit. Picking the dog up in my scope, I made a barking sound with my mouth, he stopped, and the 55-grain boattail hollow point bullet ended the unfolding drama.

This hunt took place many years ago in the rough, broken country that bordered the Niobrara River in north central Nebraska. I was testing out some new calling sounds that were on cassette tapes and were played in the Johnny Stewart electronic game call. They were mighty fine calls, and I used the heck out of them in many states across the U.S. They were heavier and bulkier than what most people use today, but they were very effective.

The first predator that I ever called in and shot was a gray fox in Virginia, over 50 years ago. I was using one of the old Bounty Hunter calls, one that played when you inserted a 45-rpm record in it. Electronic game calling has sure advanced since those days.

Before I elaborate more on the use of electronic predator calls, let me say that there will always be a need and use for handheld and mouth-blown calls. Like many other good predator men, I use both. I may be a bit overly critical when I say this, but I believe that anyone who wants to become a real pro at calling predators must be a master in the use of both. Many times I have used my old cow-horn coyote howler to locate coyotes (or let them know I'm in the area) and then used the electronic caller to bring them into my sights.

Being that I was obsessed with calling predators and other game since I was a very young lad, I have used most every brand, make or model that has been produced in the past half century. Nearly all of them would call in coyotes or other predators when used properly. Some of the calls were of very high quality, some were mediocre and a few were junk. The same goes for the calling sounds that they produce.

I still do host predator and coyote calling seminars these days, but not nearly as many as I used to. My old, worn-out body does not take well to long hours on my feet or chasing white lines down the highways for hundreds of miles anymore. I am constantly being asked by students and "wanna be" coyote killers what equipment and calls I use myself. I will not recommend any product that I haven't used and tested extensively. Nor will I lie about a product just because some manufacturer gives me freebies to use and promote.

There are many electronic game callers on the market today, ranging from very cheap in price to very expensive. In my humble opinion, the best electronic callers out there today, for the money, are those made by Icotec Game Calls. I've tested them under varied conditions (along with others) and they are what I now use. There are calls on the market that are far more expensive, and they are good, but no better, in my opinion, than the Icotec.

There are several key factors that I look at when evaluating any electronic predator call. The quality of the speaker is one. Is it clear?

Free of static? Another factor that is important is the quality of the sounds to be used. Are they real recordings? Are they clear and will they prompt a coyote to respond? I also want a caller that is compact, lightweight and tough as nails.

Most of the better calls on the market today come with a remote control device that is worth its weight in gold—if it works well! Hands down, the Icotec remote systems are by far the best I've ever used, even the one that comes with their eighty-dollar call. Please be aware of the fact that it is not my intent to knock anyone's product; I'm just stating honestly what my field tests have proven to me. If a better remote system appears on the market, I will gladly toot it to the high heaven, regardless of who made it.

The finest electronic caller made with 200 or more sounds on it will not make anyone a competent coyote killer, alone. The popularity of predator calling has grown by leaps and bounds since I first started, and in the past few years, thousands of electronic callers have hit the fields and woods and probably scared more predators than they ever called! Why? Because many of the users never really took the time to learn how to use them properly. There are really no miracles or foolproof gear to use in any kind of hunting. You must first learn how to hunt.

I have never seen the need for having hundreds of different sounds on an electronic caller. There certainly is nothing wrong with having them available, but it is not a must to be successful. For many years, all across this country, coyote control men such as myself have called in and killed thousands of coyotes with nothing more than a howler and one or two different mouth calls. I'm not telling you this to belittle electronic callers—they have their place and I like to use them. I'm telling you this to emphasize the importance of knowing your hunting territory, the quarry you seek and other skills that are needed to be successful. High tech can be a great aid for the coyote caller, but it will never replace common sense, competence and the persistence to always observe and learn from the coyote or experienced coyote callers.

One great advantage in using an electronic caller versus a hand-held, mouth-blown call is that the caller can be placed away from the hunter. An incoming coyote will focus on the area exactly where the sound is coming from, not on the shooter, which ups the odds against the critter "picking off" the shooter because of movement. I generally place my electronic caller about 40–50 feet away from my concealed position and a little to the left or right of me.

Some electronic callers now are designed to connect visual at-tractors to it (twirling, jumping, fur, feathers, etc.), and this is icing on the cake, for sure. Using one of the visual attractors may make the difference in whether a spooky coyote will come in close enough for a kill or not. Icotec has a new system out that is hard to beat for this sort of setup.

Always be alert and expect the unexpected when calling coy-otes and other predators. Quite a few years ago I was calling gray fox using a gray fox pup distress tape in some rough, broken, rocky country in New Mexico. After a few minutes of calling, I spotted a gray fox headed my way just off to my right. Before getting my gun up to the ready position I spotted movement to my left out of the corner of my eye. A full-grown, tawny mountain lion was sneaking in on that side! In the end, I became quite flustered and never killed either one!

*Bob Taylor hoists a young coyote that I called in on
his farm with the aid of my old cow horn howler.*

*The day's hunt is over, Blair survived the coyote attack and here
I am mouth howling to see if I could get a response. I did.*

CHAPTER 24

The Attack Coyote, Gerry Blair,
The Fuzz & Willis Kent

I COULD HEAR THE FOOT PADS of the coyotes drumming on the hard Arizona desert floor as they raced towards us, looking for an easy meal of rabbit. Two of them burst into the opening about 30 yards from me, and I put them in a pile with two shots from the 12-gauge. Gerry Blair, standing with his back to a greasewood bush, muttered something that was not fully understandable, but I did pick up on the word "hog."

Most of my life as a hunter and trapper in the wilds of America has been spent alone. I wanted it that way. I like people in general, but when I go to the woods, I cherish being quiet and alone. When chasing after coyotes, I rarely take anyone with me. Some of them get in the way, and some talk too much and constantly interrupt my thought process and concentration on catching coyotes. Some have labeled me as anti-social, but I don't believe I am. I'm just a little selfish when it comes to my time in the woods. Either way, it really doesn't bother me about how most people label me or what they think. I'm a happy woodsbum.

Occasionally I have hooked up for brief forays with other true coyoteros and have both learned more about coyotes and enjoyed the excursions. Gerry Blair of Flagstaff, Arizona, has been a noted authority on calling predators for decades and was a blast to hunt

Fuzz, the Montana coyote decoy dog. The best coyote dog I ever hunted with.

with. Gerry was a hard hunter and very serious when he needed to be. He was a prankster and a genuine smart ass at times, and we had a ball together. I don't think anyone has ever known more about killing Arizona coyotes and other predators with any sort of game call than Gerry Blair.

Blair and I would take turns doing the calling, and we both called and killed about the same number of coyotes. He was impressed with my use of a mouth diaphragm call back in the days when it was unheard of. I was impressed with the big galoot's knowledge and savvy on calling game, especially coyotes.

At one stop we had set up well out of sight of the truck, and it was Blair's turn to call. He cut loose with a round of pitiful squalls with his favorite call, an old Circe. After about the third call I glimpsed a yote darting through the brush, heading wide open, straight for Blair. Old Gerry let go of a few heart-wrenching moans with the Circe and all of a sudden the coyote had my partner by the pants leg. If I hadn't been there, I probably wouldn't have believed such a thing could happen.

Blair was yelling and kicking at the coyote, and I broke up laughing at the sight — a thirty-pound coyote hanging on to the leg of a 200–plus-pound screaming man! I couldn't shoot for obvious reasons. Gerry finally kicked free of the coyote, but the critter dived right back on him. By this time, I was down on my knees laughing so hard that tears ran down my face. I couldn't see for laughing, but I heard Blair's 10-gauge (he called it Moosedick) roar and I looked up to see parts of coyote flying everywhere. Blair gave the coyote and me a cussing I'll long remember. I will always cherish the memories of time spent with Gerry Blair.

I have at times turned down much-needed money from guys who wanted to pay to go with me and learn. It wasn't that I am selfish or don't want to help someone else. I just didn't think that I could stand being with some people for several days, from sunup 'til dark. I have never thought of myself as the best or the greatest anyway and wondered if I was worth their hard-earned money. The ones that I did take appeared to be satisfied in the end, but I guess I'm just too much of a loner for that kind of work or service.

Willis Kent (deceased) of Montana was another old coyotero that I thoroughly enjoyed spending time with. He was a soft-moving, quiet sort of guy who would never talk anyone to death. When he spoke, he had something worthwhile to say, and if you listened, you'd learn something. Willis roamed from Montana to New Mexico and Arizona, trapping and calling coyotes and other furbearers. It was how he made his living as long as I knew him. At one time, like myself, he would guide hunters in the fall to supplement his income. But again, like myself, he tired of spending that much time with people and gave up guiding and outfitting.

Willis owned the first coyote decoy dog that I had ever seen or hunted with. Fuzz was the pooch's name, and he was a crackerjack to say the least. Willis would make a stop where he figured or knew that coyotes laid up, give a howl with his mouth or hit the siren mounted on his truck, and we'd listen for a reply. When we got one, along with Fuzz we would move in closer and set up to call.

Fuzz sat close to Willis as he called, looking and listening. When the dog knew a coyote or coyotes were near (long before we would know), he would bristle up and whine. His master would give the command to go get them, and Fuzz would leave in a rush. Willis and I would ready our guns to shoot. Seldom were we ever disappointed by the Fuzz. He would soon have one or more coyotes on his butt and come straight to us. What a masterful play and exhibition of skill it was! I often have wondered how many coyotes old Willis and Fuzz took as a team. I doubt if Willis could have told me. He was a supreme coyote man but never bothered with numbers or bragging, and he could kill just about any coyote that needed it.

Willis and I would leave his home in Lewistown an hour or more before daylight and drive to a sprawling ranch on the Judith River where we were working on coyotes that were sneaking on to a game preserve. The owner had all sorts of exotic goats, sheep, deer and elk in thousands of fenced-in acres. The coyotes had developed a taste for the sheep and goats, costing the folks a goodly sum of money.

Normally we would make a few calls for coyotes before checking and setting traps. Fuzz was always on the truck, ready to go, well before we ate breakfast. Mrs. Kent always had a large cooler chock-full of good eats ready for us each morning. There were no stores or restaurants where we operated.

One morning I noticed Willis putting one of those old-timey hand drills on the truck and couldn't figure out how this related to coyote control. When I asked about it, the old coyote man just grinned and said, "You'll see."

At one point along the chain link fence perimeter, a large four-foot road pipe went under the roadway and fence at a deep gully. Tracks showed how coyotes were using the pipe to access the preserve and the tasty sheep. It took a while, but Willis and I managed to drill several holes in each end of the pipe. The holes were used to fasten snare support wires and the anchored end of the snare itself. By using debris to block the middle of each end of the pipe, we were able to hang two snares on each end. What a setup! We hung several coyotes in the next week at this location. As I've said before, a serious coyotero has to be adaptable and have the ability to think things through.

I spent many memorable days with Willis under that beautiful Montana sky. Deer, both whitetail and mule deer, were everywhere. It was not unusual to count over a hundred on any day. While sitting on the tailgate one day, eating lunch, we spotted three or four bull elk working their way towards us. I dropped down into a nearby sand wash with camera in hand and worked my way towards them. Willis made a few calls to get their attention. At one time I had all of those trophy bulls within 30 yards of me. I took some decent photos of them, and the real kicker was that one of the bulls was almost solid white!

To follow in the footsteps of coyoteros such as Gerry Blair, Willis Kent and some others is an honor indeed. These were men who had been up the creek and over the mountain and seen the varmint. Now I'm an old timer. I've been a sort of fledging writer for many years, but cannot find the words to aptly describe much of what I've been blessed to see.

Long live the coyoteros!

Author's Note: Since writing this piece, Gerry Blair passed away. I'm sure that if anyone is calling coyotes in the great beyond, Gerry and Willis will be right in the middle of it. These two men were the real deal.

Coyotes are fast learners and become difficult to trap, snare or call easily.

CHAPTER 25

Hard To Catch Coyotes

BETWEEN THE COYOTES and a couple of big, dog-red foxes, fifteen lambs and twenty-plus big Rhode Island Red hens had been killed on the small farm. The owners were desperate, and I was called in to stop the killing. You never know what you will have to deal with on these jobs. Some are pretty straightforward and simple, some turn into a trapper's nightmare. Some almost make you wish you'd never gotten the call.

Spring had fully arrived when I went to this farm. The red fox pups were already eating large amounts of food and the female coyotes were nursing litters. The male coyotes were scouring the countryside for food to feed the ever-hungry females. The weather was turning warm, which sometimes makes trapping canines a bit harder.

What really gave me a bad feeling was that I soon learned that a couple of beginning trappers had already attempted to catch the predators with no success. Hot weather, educated canines and livestock roaming over all the pastures spell tough going, even disaster in many situations such as this one.

I convinced the owners to move all of the sheep (along with several horses) into two pastures, which would allow me to work freely in one pasture that bordered a grown-up farm. I was sure this would be where the predators would be laying up and denning. Everything else around the farm was wide open country. I advised them of what I would charge for my services and also stated that I could not guarantee killing all of the predators. I felt pretty confident that I could stop the killing, for awhile anyway. I like to be honest and up front with folks I'm working for. I explained to them that by following after trappers who weren't really competent predator men, my job would be much harder.

The first day I put in several dirt sets with footholds but knew that I was probably wasting my time. That assumption proved to be correct when I saw both fox and coyote tracks in the dusty sheep paths that showed that the predators trotted right by the sets, showing no interest at all. I cruised about every foot of the border fence lines but did not find anywhere the varmints were coming under or through the woven wire on my first trip around. I hung snares in some of the sheep paths.

Darkness set in and I headed home. I wasn't thrilled over my prospects of doing well on this job. Years of experience gives a man gut feelings about such things. I vowed to look harder the next day for anything that could hopefully help me in doing my job. These sorts of situations put pressure on an ADC man who has a good reputation for getting the job done. Fur trapping has always been less stressful to me, even when going for big number catches. At least all of your eggs aren't in one basket on one place.

I arrived on the job at daybreak the next morning and had a large red fox in one of the snares in a sheep path. Nothing else. I pulled my truck up to the top of the hill where I could get a good view of the entire farm and just sat for awhile and looked over everything good with my binoculars. On the second look around the perimeter fence line I noticed a large oak tree with some brush growing around it and decided to look that spot over closely.

The backside of the tree was about two feet out from the fence and along with the brush had blocked my view of about six or eight

"The Lagman Coyote"

Coyotes can become shy of the trapper's sets quickly

feet of fence when I drove by it the day before. Directly behind the tree was a shallow crawl hole under the fence. Wasting no time, I hung a snare here and began to feel much better. Something would soon happen here, for sure. I checked all of the fence lines again and did hang a snare on a hole in a cross fence, which never produced a catch.

The next morning, I found a large (41-pound) male coyote in the snare back of the tree. I was mighty glad to see this old sheep eater. I was very thankful for my catch. I reset and went home. There was never any action at the dirt sets.

I was somewhat surprised the next day to find another red fox in the location where I'd caught the coyote the night before. Apparently the strong smell left by the coyote didn't kill the fox's appetite for lamb or red chickens. All of the sets went dead for a couple of days after that.

A new crawl under hole then appeared about 10' from the hole where I'd caught the coyote and red fox. A snare went in and produced another coyote, a male, that night. The traps and snares remained empty for another six or seven nights, so I pulled up. The killing ceased, the owners were happy and I was well paid. Most important of all to me, my reputation as a predator control man was still intact. I have found that no matter how good you may be overall, some people are quick to badmouth you if the opportunity arises.

Most ADC canine trappers usually wind up working for the same livestock producers year after year. Good ones knock the coyote population down pretty good and save a lot of livestock from being killed and eaten. The coyotes, being survivors, bounce back yearly. Some problem coyotes, especially the older ones, never get caught or killed. Don't ever believe that there are coyote "wizards"out there who always kill them all. That just doesn't happen, no matter how good the coyotero is. As humans with egos, we don't like to admit that some of them are too smart, too cautious or too shy for us to catch or kill. I have observed over the years that the smarter coyotes just up and leave an area for awhile when the pressure is great upon them.

It has been my experience that when dealing with hard-to-catch coyotes, I have to change tactics or fail at my job. Typical hole sets with urine, lure and bait will catch the young or others that have never seen or smelled the workings of a trapper. The same goes for flat sets using the same old lure and bait. But the older, savvy ones trot right by these sets.

Over the years, much emphasis has been put on lure and bait sets and I see less about blind sets. Snares and foothold sets (blind) in the right places are deadly coyote takers. The problem is, many trappers today, especially younger ones, have no clue on where these set locations are. It takes time in the coyote's domain and keen observation to learn about these locations. Many trappers, looking for a quicker, easier way, will not put the time in needed to develop these skills. As a consequence, they will only catch maybe a third of the coyotes in an area and never realize how many they left behind. And remember that many of those left behind have become much wiser, making them harder to catch.

I could easily write a book on blind setting for coyotes. Perhaps a knowledgeable coyote pro should do this. Lots of coyotes are snared every year at holes in fences. But if you take the average fence snare guy away from the wire, he is lost. Most will never know how to consistently catch coyotes in snares or footholds (blind) in any sort of terrain. This can easily separate the pros from the "wannabes."

Most of the coyotes I deal with on a year-around basis are hard-to-catch coyotes, with the exception of the fall pups. On occasions I am called to a place that has never been trapped, and on the first go-around most of the coyotes are easier to catch than foxes, even the old ones. But this soon changes; the survivors learn quickly.

In my line of work, I have learned that I must use every tool and method available to stop hard-to-catch coyotes from killing (as much as possible). At my age, I hesitate to invest a large sum of money in night vision optics for calling and killing coyotes at night. But being as everybody and his brother have taken up predator calling, day and night, calling in hard-to-catch coyotes has become tough in some areas. I've had to go the extra mile to get an edge. If I can't catch the killers in a trap or snare, I'll ambush them at night by using different calls or hunting over bait.

Dealing with hard-to-catch-or-kill coyotes gives the best of coyote men a real challenge at times. Sometimes I savor the challenge, sometimes I hate it. But I, like other hard-core coyote men, rarely give up. It's what we are—it's what we do.

A Jefferson coyote. Did he eat the poodle?

CHAPTER 26

Jefferson's Coyotes

I HAD DEALT A PRETTY SEVERE BLOW to the calf-killing coyotes in the rolling farm country east of where I live on my last coyote job and took a day off to regroup. Then I headed the truck south and west to the mountain country where the devilish coyotes had stirred up some folks in a bad way. No rest for the old trapper.

Poplar Forest is a big spread once owned by the famous Thomas Jefferson, one of our founding fathers. Thousands of tourists flock to the place yearly to gawk at and admire old Tommy's handiwork and architecture. Quite a few roadways and trails cut through the place, allowing folks to walk and take it all in. Pets are allowed as long as they are on a leash.

Seems like an elderly lady was walking one of the back trails with her poodle on a leash and ran into the big bad wolf, just as Little Red Riding Hood once did. A bold and somewhat brazen coyote jumped from the tall weeds adjacent to the path and put the bite on the poodle, trying to run away with it. The poor old lady yelled and screamed but held on to the leash. The coyote let go of the poodle and fled away. Although bitten severely, the poodle lived, and I'm sure the lady ruined a pair of undergarments.

Much of the land on the old plantation was still being farmed for hay by a fellow who leased the farming rights. Upon arrival, I started scouting the farm lanes and fields, setting traps here and

there at what I thought would be travel lanes or routes for the ma-
rauding pack of "wolfies." If memory serves me correctly, I put in
a dozen or so sets, more than I normally would if I had trapped
here before. It wouldn't take me long to determine where the key
locations were.

The leaves on the hardwoods had turned colors much more in
this high country than where I'd just finished trapping. The air was
cooler, and a hint of coming frost was in the air. This is the kind of
weather that makes old hounds and trappers feel much younger and
more alive. In several areas I put signs out to advise people that traps
were set in the area and to keep themselves and their pets away. The
folks running the place put out a bulletin also on my activities. I sure
as heck didn't want to be catching any pampered, high-dollar dogs.

The next day I set traps on a neighboring property that was a
high-dollar condo project surrounded by brush, fields and woods.
One lady had spotted a coyote sitting on the edge of the lawn
watching her play with her housecat on the patio. An elderly couple,
walking a nature trail down by a lake, had come face to face with a
coyote and nearly lost it. On both of these places, the trapper was a
very popular and well-liked guy (for a change).

The next morning, I had a big, dog coyote on Jefferson's place.
He was caught at a flat set made up against a large clump of fescue
grass alongside a farm road going across a hay field. I do remember
using a glob of coyote gland scent at this set. Another coyote, one of
this year's pups, was caught about 200 yards away where the farm
road entered the woods. Over at the condo project, I had caught an
elder female in a trap set on the lake dam. Not 30 yards from the
female coyote, I had a gray fox in another trap.

Catching the gray was a bonus. I sold live foxes to the dog running pens, getting $40.00 for grays and $60.00 for reds. I had to
caution myself against getting a little cocky or biggity with my success. As long as I've been trapping, I knew for a fact that things

Another of the
Jefferson culprits.

could go the other way just as well. I showed the critters to the managers (who hired me) at both places and received the typical handshakes and slaps on the back. For a little while, at least, I was somebody's hero; I wanted them to see I was doing my job.

That afternoon I pushed on to a place about 35 miles north where I was needed. A very exclusive, high-dollar retreat was experiencing problems with skunks. Seems like a guest from somewhere in Europe had spotted a skunk digging for grubs in the lawn and thought it was a housecat. Approaching the "cat" to pet it, the poor soul got it good. These kinds of incidents could prove disastrous for such a place. Also, the building and grounds manager had twice spotted a coyote or coyotes slinking around.

A bit of searching on my part soon turned up two active skunk dens, one in an old groundhog den in a nearby hedgerow. The other was found where they were living under an equipment shed. I set two cubbies (wooden) with 155 or 160 killer traps a few feet out from the hole, baited with my rank homemade fish bait, at each location. To-morrow I would bring three or four live cage traps to set at locations closer to the lawn area where the skunks were feasting on grubs.

I put in two coyote sets on the far side of the hedgerow and headed home. This trapline would require about 150 miles of driving a day, and I sure didn't like that part of it. Due to old age, arthritis and previous bone breakages, both my knees and one hip give me a lot of grief when I sit and drive for any length of time. An old fool must love trapping to suffer through some of the worse days and still keep at it.

Several times in recent years I've thought of retiring—quitting. I can't seem to go through with it. Starting this fall, I've been trapping for 60 years. Trapping has been my love, my life. It has often afforded me a living doing what I like to do. I've seen a lot of trappers and a heap of "wannabes" come and go. I also know a few who have trapped longer than I have, and with those men I feel a real bonding. A true-blue, dyed-in-the-wool trapper has to trap.

After about a week's trapping, I ended up catching four coyotes off of Jefferson's Poplar Forest. Two more were caught on the condo place. I also caught four or five fox, which added to my overall earnings, above and beyond what I was getting paid. The sets went dead, except for an occasional gray fox trying to dig at the side or back of a set. I never took the time to slip in an extra trap or two to catch the little gray devils.

At the mountaintop, high-dollar retreat I caught a dozen or so skunks. Most were caught in the baited killer/cubby sets. I found that the little 155s did a real job on the skunks, killing them quickly. A little of the rank essence would dribble out, but I never had one really spray. The skunks caught in the cage traps were carefully moved and hauled away. One day some of the folks there videoed me loading one up. They sure were impressed and nicknamed me "The Skunk Whisperer." I'm sure I've been called worse names.

On a walkabout below the hedgerow and beyond where the coyote traps were set, I came up on several remains of skunks and one possum. It dawned on me then why the coyotes had been seen so close by. They were preying on the skunks! I should have thought of that in the beginning, but at times I'm a slow learner. There is a reason why any wild animal goes anywhere or does anything. We just have to be smart enough to see it or figure it out. Wildlife of all kinds do not have the luxury that we have to idle time away.

I finally connected with a double on coyotes, a male and a female, by the hedgerow on the fourth or fifth night. The folks who ran the place were awed by the coyotes and happy to see them gone, but I was thinking that maybe they would have been better off leaving the coyotes. They were eating the skunks and didn't get any pay for it! The male coyote was a big 'un, weighing in at a few ounces under 50 pounds.

No more coyotes were caught at this place, and I figured that this pair came on their own, away from the pack, to hog the skunk meat. They may have been part of a family or a pack, but survival is paramount to all of them. The survival of the fittest theory is deeply ingrained into them.

Many folks, even some trappers, think that coyotes always travel or hunt in a pack, but this is not so. They will spread out singularly or in small groups to hunt and then pack up again when they desire to do so. That is one of the reasons why we sometimes catch only one or two of them in an area where we have more traps set. Some we will never catch.

I was glad to see this trapline come to a successful end. The driving alone had worn me down. Not to mention the fact that you wear out an expensive truck in a hurry with putting all of those miles on it each day. Several calls had come in with jobs closer to home and I was ready for them.

One of 97 coyotes taken from a 1200-acre sheep and cattle farm in a 4½-year period by James Southall. James is becoming a coyote specialist. The 50-plus-pound coyote he's holding will more than likely have wolf genes in him.

CHAPTER 27

The Coyote Specialist

PART I

I T WILL TAKE A LOT MORE PHYSICAL WORK to catch 100 coyotes than one coyote, but it is sometimes simpler and less stressful to catch 100 coyotes than one. Most any coyotero that has had to deal with coyotes to any extent will, I believe, agree with the above statement. Some coyotes are very hard to catch and some will never be caught.

I don't think that there is a coyote on earth that can't be caught or killed, if a knowledgeable coyote man devotes enough time to the project. Some that can't be caught in foot traps can be snared, some that can't be snared can be called in and shot. Some can be shot over bait and some can be killed with the aid of dogs, either hounds or decoy dogs.

There is a demand now in many areas for real coyoteros—the competent specialists. As time goes on, there will be even more demand for them, especially around towns, cities, urban areas and livestock-producing country. I get quite a few calls every year now where coyotes have set up housekeeping, on a permanent basis, right in towns and subdivisions. Old wiley is very adaptable, indeed.

There are quite a few guys scattered around the U.S. who can catch a coyote or two. There are some who do a little better and catch maybe 10-50 coyotes every year, if they trap or hunt hard. There is a growing number of coyote callers who kill quite a few coyotes every year, especially those out west where coyotes are called in easier than in the east. The new breed of coyote killers in the east with their state-of-the-art electronic calling machines and their expensive night vision optics kill quite a few. But are all of these guys expert coyote men, real coyote specialists? Hell no, by no means.

The bona fide coyote specialists are the ones who are called in after many of the others have gone through an area and trapped or killed some of the coyotes. Some of these guys trap and call several hundred places a year, and their take is often impressive. But they are usually not the guys who kill the educated, hard-to-kill coyotes. Many of these guys cannot catch or kill the older, wise ones.

I have a project coming up that should prove to be quite interesting. I would also bet you that it will prove to be somewhat stressful before it is over with. I have been called to a place where several different trappers and callers have been on for three or four years now and have killed hardly any coyotes. From what I have learned, these guys have caught and killed a few coyotes around the country, so they are not pure novices. You can bet that the coyotes that travel through this place, at least the older ones, have seen every hole and flat set known to man! I'll bet they can sniff a scent or lure and tell you what brand it is. And I'll wager that these coyotes will not even break stride when they see a typical coyote set, not even to pee on it.

Because I have trapped many livestock-producing farms, the same ones, for several years running, I have to deal with the wise, educated ones. When a man pays you to stop the killings and thin down the coyotes, you have to produce or lose face. Your reputation as a coyotero can go to hell in a handbasket in a hurry. A coyote specialist is always under stress as a rule, and his work is much more involved than the guy who pulls up his traps after catching nothing for a week and moves to a place where the coyotes are still naïve to the games that trappers or callers play.

On one farm, not too long ago, I was dealing with a few coyotes that were killing a calf a week, just like clockwork. Having trapped

*The author with a morning's take of coyotes that were killing
and harassing livestock. Once coyotes learn about traps,
snares and calls, it takes a specialist to remove them.*

this place for three or four years, I knew where all of the typical, "hot" locations to set traps or hang snares were. After making five or six typical sets at these locations, I then started looking for a place or two where I could really catch the coyotes. I made the typical sets for several reasons. One, I knew there was always a chance of catching a three-fourths-grown pup at one of these sets, and some-times I'd catch a red or gray fox that I could sell alive to the running pens—a bonus for my efforts, you might say.

I spent at least two hours cruising around the perimeter fence, looking and thinking. Thinking is probably the most important thing in a coyote specialist's arsenal. I have been with trappers who are really good at picking typical locations, and they could pound in a typical coyote set before I even got my leather gloves on. But they were not thinkers and keen observers. They could honestly be called coyote trappers, but they would never make specialists.

Finally, somewhat frustrated, I hung one snare on a barbwire fence next to a corner brace post. I had spotted three or four guard hairs left on a barb by a coyote. On the other side of the pasture, I made two well-blended-in blind sets in a well-used cow path that bordered the fence. Had there been any brush, weeds or cover what-soever along the path, I would have hung a snare or two. But there wasn't, and I knew that these older coyotes traveling the cow path would have simply left the path and gone around my exposed loops. Tracks in dust, mud and snow have shown me many times in the past when old wiley pulled these stunts. Not all of them are stupid. Also, I didn't want to snare a cow or calf by the foot.

I checked this place for a week, catching a gray fox, two coons and one skunk in the conventional baited and lured sets. The two blind set foot traps set in the cow path had been set off twice by cows, but I knew this would happen when I set them, so I just bit the bullet and kept resetting them. The snare in the fence was still hanging, untouched.

On the eighth or ninth day, I could see a dead Angus calf out in the pasture, with the mama cow standing off to the side, mooing her head off. She had created a circular trail around her dead offspring. There was nothing left of the calf but feet, head and some hide. I was not a happy trapper, and I knew there was going to be an unhappy cow man also.

Disgusted, I rode on to check my sets. The conventional sets were all empty, but the snare in the fence held a large, male coyote. Since I was using non-locking, non-kill locks on my snares and the coyote hadn't hung himself in the fence, I shot the killer with my .22 pistol. While he was doing his death kicks, I rode up the fence-line to check the sets on the other side. The first blind set had a tripped off trap (damn cows!) sitting in the bed, and the other held a mature coyote, a female. Things were surely looking up for this old trapper and the future calf crop.

The sets were remade and left for another week with no catches, other than a coon. We lost no other calves on that farm that fall.

These are the sort of situations that separate the average coyote killer from the coyote specialist. Many trappers do not have the patience, nor the ability, to adapt to methods that will get the job done. I have, through necessity and desire, learned a little on how to deal with different coyote situations. So if I can, I figure that most any other coyote man can do the same, but you really have to WANT TO DO IT!

The two coyotes killing the calves on that farm had apparently made their kill, filled up on veal and were caught when leaving the pasture. The cow man was not happy about losing the last calf (or any of the previous ones), but he was more than willing to pay for my efforts. And my reputation as a real coyotero specialist was still intact!

Cattle and sheep farmer Susan Swales holds a sheep killing coyote I caught on her place. It took some time to get him.

CHAPTER 28

The Coyote Specialist

PART II

SEVERAL FACTORS OVER THE PAST 20 YEARS or so drove or coaxed me into becoming more and more of a coyote specialist. One of those factors was that coyotes had invaded the East after I moved back here from New Mexico, and there were few people around who knew much about killing or catching them. I found myself in a position where people were willing to pay me good money to trap and kill coyotes, year around. That's sort of like throwing a hog into a 500-gallon tub of slop!

Another factor that drove me somewhat into the coyote specialty was that of age and physical condition. Sometime around when I was 55-60 years old, I realized that catching, toting, skinning and putting up 10-12 beaver a day, along with other fur, was not as fun as it was when I was a young buck, full of pee and vinegar. The aches, the pains, the constant fatigue and the daily falls in beaver swamps took the fun right out of it. I have hundreds of fond memories of trapping a few thousand beaver and a heap of otter over the years, but my old bones won't take much of it anymore. Not meaning to make any trapper out there feel bad, but I do believe the average, high-rolling beaver trapper has to be a bit retarded!

The third factor that pushed me further towards becoming a coyote specialist was that as I trapped coyotes around the country, and others started catching a few also, the coyotes began wising up! Sure, at first it was no big deal to go out and catch a few coyotes anywhere. Most of them worked a set aggressively and didn't know what a trap or snare was. But time changed all of that. After a while, most of the coyote control work that I was getting was on places where coyotes had been messed with before. These situations often prove to be very challenging, to say the least.

A true coyote specialist has to be good with traps, snares and predator calls. At some point in time, anything that can be used to catch or kill a coyote will have to be put into play. I spent a good many years in many western states hunting and trapping coyotes with some of the best coyote men that ever put a pair of britches on. Some of these guys are long gone, and they were never famous on a national level. But they were sure praised and revered by cow and sheep ranchers in their area of operations. All of these men, every one of them, were proficient with traps, snares and calls. Most of them were experts at howling coyotes. The majority of them used, or had used, decoy and denning dogs.

I have never known an expert coyote specialist that was not a thinking man. I learned from them that you often have to think your way through catching a particularly wise coyote. Smart people have been telling us for years that humans never use but a small part of their brains, but I believe that some coyotes I have dealt with use all of their brain power and some borrowed from others. I have watched men like Willis Kent of Montana pull up to a place to trap and just sit, look and think for a long time.

Being young, I would be anxious to jump out of the truck and pound in two traps here, two over there and hang a snare in every opening. Willis never really tried to discourage me from my hyped-up frame of mind. He would just walk around, look carefully at what was there and then stand and think a bit more. Sometimes I could hear him chuckling at me. I probably set three traps or snares

Another summertime livestock killer that
gave me a real run for the money.

to every one that Willis set. I would often ask him, "Do you think this is a good location?"

"Yep, I'd say you could catch a coyote there. You set that place and I'll set one over here."

Willis always caught or snared three times more coyotes than I did. Somewhere back in those long-ago times, I finally realized that I needed to spend as much or more time thinking and looking than I did setting traps. I really started paying attention to what those old coyoteros were thinking and doing. A lot of things that I learned from them will never be seen printed in books or put on videos.

Patience is a virtue that is an absolute must for an expert coyote specialist. We have been bombarded over the past 30-40 years with the teachings of many "high rollers" who catch thousands of critters, never miss a one and they do all of this very quickly. It has often become a numbers game. While some of these fellows have caught a lot of animals, even coyotes, few of them ever become coyote specialists. They simply do not have the patience to become one!

As a younger man, I did learn much about patience and trapping when I chased after mink and otter. Assess your territory, set the best locations and wait! If you have looked things over carefully, thought it all out and set your traps accordingly, a bit of patience will sooner or later show you an animal in the trap. Coyotes travel a lot. They don't always walk the same path or road every trip through a place. They don't always go under or through a fence at the same place. They are not always hungry. You have to be patient to catch the wiley ones.

Speaking of numbers, even as worn out as I am now, I can catch and kill 1,000 or more coyotes in my area (covering two or three counties) in a year if I choose to do so. Now some would find that hard to believe. Some will laugh at me. But the coyotes are here. For any coyote specialist who can trap, snare and call coyotes anywhere, anytime of the year, this is not such a hard feat to accomplish. That's a little less than three coyotes per day. I don't do it simply because people won't pay me to do it, and a man would go broke trapping coyotes just for fur in this part of the country, even when furs are prime. Also, as I grow older, I don't have a burning ego that drives me, nor do I care to kill but so many animals. The only times now that I have anything to prove to anybody is when I have to stop coyotes from killing their livestock, chickens or pets. Age mellows most of us.

I have mentioned on several occasions that a coyote specialist needs to be a good coyote caller. When I say a good coyote caller, I'm referring to a caller who can call them in with both mouth-blown and electronic callers, day or night. A coyote man who's good with a howler (mouth-blown) and knows coyote lingo can put a lot of stock killers in the grave that are hard to catch or kill using traps and snares. I have an old horn howler, made by Herb Brusman from Oregon, that I've used for years; it has accounted for many a coyote. He and his daughter-in-law still make and sell them. Herb is an old-time coyote specialist who sent many of them to coyote heaven.

So many coyotes in the east have been educated to calls (screaming rabbit, etc.) by "Bubbas" and wannabes who have bought electronic calls and didn't learn to do things right before they used them. I do use an Icotec electronic call with different sounds at times, and it's as good a caller as money can buy. As a whole, I still prefer mouth-blown calls and the howler.

You can be a coyote specialist if you really want to be. There is a future in it, believe me. I'm not the authority on the subject, but this old coon has been there and done that. As I have said previously, numbers don't impress me like they used to. In the past we have had some really good numbers men and we have some today. My hat's off to them, but I can't hack it like I used to.

But now when I catch that crafty old coyote that no one else before me could, I have to admit that I still swell a bit from pride. I thank God that he has let me be a woodsbum and trapper!

All four of these differently colored coyotes came out of the same county.

CHAPTER 29

Coyote Colors

I COULD SEE A YELLOW-COLORED ANIMAL moving around where I had set a trap on the other side of a fencerow, and my first thought was that I'd caught a feral dog. In the east, these devils of mixed ancestry come in most any color and size you can imagine. They are a scourge on the land, killing and eating anything they can catch to survive. Coyotes often get blamed for what these mongrels kill.

Upon pulling up to the trapped animal I was surprised to see a large, blonde-colored coyote. Before this I had caught most any color of coyote you can imagine—brown, gray, silver, black, red and various combinations of all of these colors. But the coloring on this one was truly unique for me. The fur on the pelt was long and silky, since it was caught in December when coyote hides or pelts are "prime." I had the pelt tanned and it now hangs in my den along with others of various colors.

In many areas of North America where I have taken or studied coyotes, about all of them are of the same color in that particular area. In some areas they are a brownish color, in other areas they are a mix of gray and silver. I believe that coyotes with mostly the same color in an area are more than likely a pure strain of coyotes. All of the coyotes I've ever seen have lighter-colored belly fur, some almost white.

I was trapping on another farm about fifteen miles from where I caught the blonde one the same year and caught a solid black coyote.

A very unusual colored coyote.

Three or four other coyotes caught on this particular farm were all a silver/gray color with white belly fur. In the area where I took the blonde coyote, I caught others that were different colors. Some were mostly brown and some were gray. For the past few years I have attempted to take a photo of every coyote I catch for two reasons. One, about all of my coyote work is damage control work, and I like to show the landowners or stockmen what I have taken on their properties. They can see that they are getting their money's worth. Secondly, I like to keep records for my coyote studies and research. Sometimes I have to look through the hundreds of coyote photos saved on my computer (my wife has to help me on this) to pick out a photo or two for a magazine article. I am amazed at how coyote colors are so varied.

Many of us who have spent much time chasing after and observing wildlife have seen firsthand how The Creator colored many forms of life so they would blend in with their habitat and surroundings. The reason for this was to aid them in survival, both predators and prey. Coyotes (pure strains) in sagebrush country have fur colors that blend in with the sage. Coyotes living in other types of habitat have colors that most often blend in with the predominant colors of the landscape. Of course, there will be variables found in all things that exist in nature.

Genetics entered the coyote's world and created changes in their colors. Coyotes interbred with dogs and wolves of different colors and all bets were off. We see white wolves and black wolves, along with gray and brownish ones. We see dogs of almost every color on the chart. Once the gene pool was tampered with and purity was lost, we have coyotes of all colors. We can expect most anything. I have yet to catch a black and white "pinto" coyote, but who knows what's out there!

Many of us old coyoteros believe that the coyote is the most intelligent mammal found in North America.

CHAPTER 30

More Observations on Coyotes

ONE BEAUTIFUL SPRING MORNING I spotted a coyote on the back edge of a hayfield as I drove along a back country road. I knew the landowner and turned around and went back to the field. Upon seeing my truck pulling into the field, the coyote took to the woods. Looking the field over, I saw the farmer at the far end of the field on his tractor, cutting hay.

I waited until the farmer came back around close to me. He stopped the tractor and came over to my truck. "I can see that the coyote man is on the job, but he's a little late," the man said with a big grin on his face. "That big devil of a coyote has been following my tractor around all morning, and I don't have a rifle with me. Why the hell is he following me around? I thought them things was supposed to be smart."

"Most of them are pretty smart," I replied. "When that haybine of yours cuts up a rabbit or a mouse, he's there to eat it. You're making his job of hunting for food much easier. By the size of him, I figure that one is a male, out hunting for himself and probably a female with pups."

"Well I'll be damned," the farmer replied. "I hope you can kill all of the devils so they won't be after my calves this fall. I lost two calves this past season to them."

Over the years I have witnessed coyotes doing this several times, and farmers are often telling me about coyotes following them around hayfields. Old wiley has learned that this is an easy way to fill his belly. This is just another example of how coyotes adapt and survive most anywhere. I know one farmer who kills a coyote or two every year by keeping a rifle on his tractor while he cuts hay.

While sitting on a high point out west one morning, glassing the country below me for deer and elk, I noticed five or six vultures take to the air and light in nearby trees. I figured the scavengers were attempting to feed on a lion or bear kill but were being run off. The trees and brush were thick in that area, and I couldn't tell what had flushed them. I continued glassing all of the area around me and soon picked up a coyote moving along a ridge in the direction of the vultures. The coyote would trot along for a spell and then stop and stare at the vultures. Soon the critter went out of sight when he dropped off the ridge into the brush. Coyotes have learned to watch the movements of buzzards and vultures. They know that there's something to eat around when they see them going to the ground. A week later I was scouting that country again and poked around in the thicket. I found what was left of a clean-picked mule deer doe. Lion tracks were spotted in a bare, sandy area nearby. Coyote scat was near the carcass along with vulture feathers. The interaction of wildlife with one another always amazes me. That one mule deer doe had helped feed three other species of wildlife.

Wiley Carroll (deceased), the legendary lion hunter and coyotero from Nevada, told me years ago that neither vultures nor coyotes will feed on a fresh lion kill for fear of the lion killing them. In areas where deer are plentiful and hunting is easy for lions, they often leave much of the meat to waste away. The lion does not care for tainted, rotted meat. Once the meat becomes spoiled, the lion will move on and the coyotes and vultures move in on it and pick the bones clean.

This coyote flattened out and attempted to hide from me.

Coyotes will eat undigested grain found in livestock droppings. They have also been seen eating the droppings of nursing calves, apparently relishing the taste of any undigested milk found in it. Trappers have opened up coyote stomachs for years to try and determine what they eat, and wildlife scientists have analyzed stomach contents and feces from coyotes to learn more about their eating habits. I don't believe we will ever learn all there is to know about a coyote's diet.

Ancient Indian cultures told stories about the relationship between coyotes and badgers. Many of them believed that they were cousins because they were sometimes seen hunting and working together to obtain food. Dr. Ed Sceery, the famed coyotero from New Mexico, told me that he had witnessed teamwork between coyotes and badgers three times in his lifetime. A badger would dig on one side of a rodent hole and when the rodent popped out the coyote would grab it. Sometimes the badger caught and ate the rodent before it managed to come out of the den or hole. Naturalist, hunter, teacher and author Frank Dobie (deceased) wrote of witnessing this happening in his book *Song of the Coyote.*

There have been many bona fide reports of coyotes and badgers traveling and hunting together. These reports have come from all over the country from people who spend much of their time studying wildlife. No one can explain this relationship between two predators. Coyotes will eat badger flesh and badgers will feed on a dead coyote, but they will sometimes play and hunt together. Strange indeed.

Another interesting story about coyotes on the hunt in urban areas was told to me by a fellow who has performed coyote control work in city and urban areas for years. He utilizes many wildlife cameras to record the habits and movements of these "city slicker" coyotes. One of his cameras recorded a video of a pair of coyotes that appeared on a sidewalk that ran through a high income neighborhood. The coyotes split up—one remained on the sidewalk while the other worked its way through and behind the shrubbery planted in front of the houses. Rodents (mostly rabbits and mice) would be flushed out from the shrubbery, and the coyote on the sidewalk would grab them! Once in a while a house cat or small dog would pop out and the coyotes had a real feast.

Normally coyotes relish eating on a dead cow. In recent years, however, I have kept an eye on cow carcasses that were never eaten on. I knew that coyotes were around, and this really had me puzzled, so I began an investigation. I talked to some sharp coyoteros all around the country and found out they had been seeing this also. Wayne Derrick of New Mexico explained to me that he had discovered that some of the powerful medications that were injected into sick cows were the reason for coyotes shying away from the flesh.

Further research confirmed what Wayne had told me. I find it truly amazing that coyotes can smell and sense such things. Now if the sick cow had lived and eventually ended up at the slaughter house, we dumb-assed humans would be eating what a coyote turned down! Makes me wonder who's the smartest.

One of twelve sheep killed in a pasture in a night's time. Only two were eaten on.

Felicia Taylor with two summer time coyotes.

CHAPTER 31

Parting Words

I TRULY HOPE THAT WHAT I HAVE SHARED with the readers of this book has helped some learn more about coyotes and understand them better. Neither I nor anyone else have all the answers to the many questions about coyotes. I don't think we ever will. The coyote seems to adapt and evolve better than any other species of wildlife I know of or have studied. They are remarkable animals.

In the very beginning of this writing, I stated that I would be critical of what many wildlife scientists, researchers, biologists and wildlife agency folks have been telling us about coyotes. In no way have I intended to be mean in my disagreements with many of them. Myself and other coyoteros have felt for a long time that many of these people needed to be questioned because we know that much of what they have been telling is simply not the truth.

It is my hope that some in the scientific and academic professions will develop the backbone to question some of their teachers. I hope that some of these people will get off their cushy cans and go to the woods, fields, deserts, prairies and mountains and really study coyotes in their element. I am hoping that these people can let go of some of their pride and egos and listen to those who really know and study coyotes in the field, day after day, year after year. Perhaps if we all worked together, we could really accomplish something good and positive.

I have said many times before that I have no hatred for coyotes. They belong here, just as we do. Yes, I have killed thousands of them, but I will never brag about this. I did what needed to be done, and someone will always be needed to control coyotes. If we do not come up with a good program to control coyotes, there will be hell to pay down the road. You can bank on that.

In the America that we live in today, so many people are caught up in being politically correct. Political correctness should have nothing to do with good wildlife management. Politicians and lawmakers at all levels of government, along with wildlife agency personnel, need to step up and do their part or be held accountable for not doing so. We have an obligation to respect, preserve and manage all wildlife. We must also realize that overly emotional animal rights people will not and cannot manage coyotes or any other species of wildlife properly. Nor can hunters, trappers, scientists and academics who are so narrow-minded and refuse to see the truth.

I have a lot of respect for the coyote. He is what he is. I really like having them around, doing the good things that coyotes do. What I don't like is attempting to deal with people who are not as smart as coyotes.

Old Wiley

I set my traps with utmost caution,
and practiced skill,
For there is a coyote around,
that I need to kill.

Some say he's just an animal,
he can't even think.
I beg to differ with these people,
Some coyotes have driven
me to strong drink.

He will crap by our traps, or
pay them no attention at all,
Just let us catch 5 out of 10,
and we stand 10 foot tall.

Man can be arrogant, he lords
over all that is wild,
But old wiley comes along, and
makes him whimper like a child.

No man alive, has ever made
all coyotes go away,
He has shown us that he
is clever, he most certainly will stay.

Other books by Don Shumaker

Follow The Dream

Sam Carns, a young trapper and hunter, leaves the Blue Ridge Mountains of Virginia in 1860 and heads west to become a mountain man, trapper and hunter. A lively tale of adventure by an author who has lived the mountain man lifestyle. Readers say that they had a hard time putting this book down!

Woodsbum

Don Shumaker chose to turn his back on the hectic, often unrewarding lifestyle that so many people fall victim to. He wrested a living from the wilds as a hunter, guide, trapper and from other outdoor pursuits. Go with him on his life's journey of 60 years doing what many men only dream of doing. This story of one man's life is inspiring to many. He has lived the life of a truly free spirit.

For more information on where you can obtain these books, contact donshu@centurylink.net or visit his Facebook - Don Shumaker, Author, Outdoorsman.